A New Vision of Family Life

A Reflection on *Amoris laetitia*

WITH A FOREWORD BY
Cardinal Blase J. Cupich

Louis J. Cameli

LTP
LITURGY
TRAINING
PUBLICATIONS

Nihil Obstat
Reverend Mr. Daniel G. Welter, JD
Chancellor
Archdiocese of Chicago
March 9, 2018

Imprimatur
Very Reverend Ronald A. Hicks
Vicar General
Archdiocese of Chicago
March 9, 2018

Excerpts from *Amoris laetitia* reprinted with the permission of Libreria Vaticana Editrice.

Excerpt from *Amoris laetitia: accompagnare, discernere e integrare la fragilità— la morale cattolica dopo il capitolo ottavo*, by Basilio Petrà, Assisi: Cittadella Editrice, 2016.

Cover design by Kari Nicholls.

22 21 20 19 18   1 2 3 4 5

Printed in the United States of America

Library of Congress Control Number: 2018937790

ISBN 978-1-61671-430-7

NVF

✺

For

Evelyn Grace Carley,

who shows us

the joy of love.

Contents

Foreword

With the publication of *Amoris laetitia*, Pope Francis urged readers to take their time to study this document in its entirety, so that it could be properly received. In this book, Father Louis Cameli demonstrates the benefits of following that sage advice. For starters, he offers us a fully integrated reading of this postsynodal apostolic exhortation. This allows him to avoid the trap of giving inordinate attention to only one chapter or topic. As such, Father Cameli stands apart from those who have focused solely on so-called irregular marriages and the issue of receiving the Eucharist, even to the point of hastily reaching conclusions based on a myopic reading of the text. By not allowing the question of the reception of *Amoris laetitia* to be limited in this way, the author gives us a full appreciation of the wide beauty and vast substance of the exhortation. All of this opens up a pathway for its implementation based on the incisive insights and pastoral imperatives found in each of the chapters.

One of the most important insights is in the first paragraphs of *Amoris laetitia*. There, Pope Francis observes that the experience of family life frames the entirety of salvation history in Sacred Scripture. He writes:

> The Bible is full of families, births, love stories, and family crises. This is true from its very first page, with the appearance of Adam and Eve's family with all its burden of violence but also its enduring strength (cf. *Gen* 4) to its very last page, where we behold the wedding feast of the Bride and the Lamb (*Rev* 21:2, 9). (*Amoris laetitia*, 8)

In a word, God has made family life the privileged place for God's self-revelation, manifesting how God acts and relates to humanity and the world.

This insight has enormous consequences for the Church's pastoral ministry to families. Rather than defining it solely in terms of applying the teachings of our tradition to the problems and challenges families face, we should consider that their lives, lived in this present moment, are also part of salvation history in which God continues to engage humanity. As such, families are not problems to solve but opportunities for the Church to discern with the aid of the Spirit how God is active in our time and what God is calling us to do here and now.

Father Cameli fully explores this seminal insight of the Holy Father as he gives a careful and thorough reading of *Amoris laetitia*. This allows him to provide a more ample and richer vision of issues related to marriage and family life, such as marriage preparation, the raising of children, and the full participation of families in the life of parishes. The goal is always the same—a pastoral approach to families that assists them to discern how God is calling and gracing them with mercy and redemption as they face their challenges and struggles, their joys and blessings, all the while enabling them to enrich the life of the Church in our time. This serves as a corrective to a narrow or reductive understanding of the role of conscience by framing it in terms of discerning the will of a generously merciful God in the particular circumstances a person faces. In this way, Father Cameli is faithful to the creative balance between doctrinal tradition and pastoral accompaniment that the pope proposes in the exhortation. Asserting without equivocation the full ideal of marriage, he takes issue with "a more rigorous pastoral care which leaves no room for confusion" (308). He offers instead a ministry to families that is marked by pastoral accompaniment, one that fully reflects the omnipotence of God, especially when it comes to God's mercy. Doing otherwise only places obstacles and conditions on God's mercy, to the point that "we empty it of its concrete meaning and real significance" (311). Father Cameli rightly highlights how this rigorist approach is neither pastorally nor doctrinally faithful to the tradition, and as Pope Francis observes with no little irony, ends up being "the worst way of watering down the Gospel" (311).

My hope is that Father Cameli's book will spark a new momentum, igniting a much needed and overdue discussion of *Amoris laetitia* among the faithful, theologians, and Church leadership in our country. Such a balanced discussion, marked by collaboration and shared wisdom, will help us avoid the trap of isolating one particular issue or section of this magisterial document. In fact, now that Pope Francis has published his letter to the Buenos Aires bishops, along with their interpretation of *Amoris laetitia* in *Acta Apostolica Sedis*, confirming that their pastoral exposition authentically reflects his mind, we have a solid point of reference as we pursue these discussions in fidelity to the official teaching of the Church on marriage and family life. In all of this, we likewise need to keep in mind what we know about interpreting magisterial teaching, namely, that when doctrine develops, earlier teachings need to be read in light of the new development. Consequently, as we study previous magisterial documents on marriage and family life, we should read them in light of the contribution of *Amoris laetitia*, a task made easier and more profound by Father Cameli's book.

Just as Father Cameli heeded the urging of Pope Francis, so should we. It is important to take our time to read and study *Amoris laetitia* alongside this helpful companion, grateful that it has been prepared by a theologian whose skill and thoughtfulness is outmatched only by his devotion to the Holy Father and his love of the Church.

—Cardinal Blase J. Cupich

1

Amoris laetitia in Context

Unity of teaching and practice is certainly necessary in the Church, but this does not preclude various ways of interpreting some aspects of that teaching or drawing certain consequences from it.

—Amoris laetitia, 4

In 2014, Pope Francis convoked an extraordinary synod of bishops to identify concerns and challenges facing marriage and family life. A second synod met in 2015 to respond to those concerns and challenges. A worldwide consultation not only with bishops but with all the faithful preceded both synodal assemblies. In the Archdiocese of Chicago, I had the responsibility to collate and synthesize the local responses. Several thousand responses came in, an extraordinary response rate that indicated the deep interest in the themes of the synods. People freely expressed the blessings that they had experienced in their marriages and families. They were grateful for the felt presence of God, who accompanied them. They were also concerned about many things that seemed to diminish their life together; for example, a culture with values that failed to support marriages and families, questions about the future faith and religious practice of their children and grandchildren, and the ways that social media had invaded the intimate circle of family life. As I read and synthesized these responses, I was deeply moved. I also realized that the Holy Father had indeed touched the center of lives and faith with his proposal for the two synods.

The result of the extensive consultation of bishops and the faithful and the two synods was Pope Francis' apostolic exhortation *Amoris laetitia, The Joy of Love: On Love in the Family*, which he presented to the world on March 19, 2016. The exhortation runs well over two hundred pages. It is addressed to bishops, priests, deacons, consecrated persons, Christian married couples, and all the lay faithful. In other words, *Amoris laetitia* is destined for the entire Church.

Many people have warmly received the exhortation as an expression of the pope's concern for marriages and family life. Others, as Cardinal Cupich indicates in his foreword, have read it narrowly. And some have found it seriously wanting. Overall, in my estimation, people have not completely understood the exhortation and, consequently, have been unable to receive it fully. Why might this be so?

Amoris laetitia represents a very new moment in magisterial teaching on marriage and the family. We are unaccustomed to its way of teaching and its implications for pastoral practice. Some historical context can help us to understand how the exhortation breaks new ground.

Before the end of the nineteenth century, theological reflection and magisterial teaching on marriage and family life had a narrow focus. Concerns centered on legal questions of consent and validity as well as on the theological question of the sacramentality of marriage. Then, in the nineteenth century, significant changes occurred in marriage and family life. Church teaching needed to develop to meet new and growing challenges.

In the nineteenth century, great shifts in family life accompanied the emergence of industrialization, urbanization, and state involvement in the social order that could extend even into the intimate circle of family life. These experiences put considerable stress on families. Church teaching on marriage and family began to respond to these challenges with Pope Leo XIII's encyclical *Rerum novarum* (1891). In that encyclical, the pope emphasized the questions of rights and justice. In the twentieth century, the availability of artificial contraception, the globalization of the economy, and the development of electronic technology added more stress on family life. Magisterial teaching began to address questions of morality—specifically, questions surrounding the use of artificial contraception. This teaching culminated in Pope

Paul VI's encyclical *Humanae vitae* (1968). Pope John Paul II developed previous teaching. In fact, Pope John Paul II's notable apostolic exhortation on family life, *Familiaris consortio* (1981), synthesized the previous magisterial teaching on marriage and family life with its treatment of doctrine, rights, morality, social analysis, and pastoral care.

Finally, in our day, Pope Francis has promulgated *Amoris laetitia* (2016). With its teaching and proposals for marriage and family life, this exhortation breaks new ground. It presumes previous magisterial teaching concerning sacramentality, the social order, rights, canon law, and morality. In an unprecedented way, *Amoris laetitia* directly addresses spiritual and moral formation. In fact, formation is at the center of its concern. This shift represents a pastoral conversion, perhaps even a revolution, in retrieving the centrality of marriage and family life in the transformative life and journey of faith for Christ's disciples.

Amoris laetitia has the potential to rewrite fundamental pastoral directions for the life of the Church. This does not mean a change in doctrine. Rather, the new directions would relocate the center of our attention and resituate pastoral efforts and energies in supporting the journey of discipleship for the People of God in marriage and family life. In a time when we can all be deeply troubled and concerned about our future as a Church,[1] *Amoris laetitia* offers us new vision and new hope.

In the chapters that follow, I try to identify the new directions for marriage and family life that *Amoris laetitia* proposes. These chapters do not provide an exhaustive commentary on this document. Rather, they are meant as a point of departure for pastoral and personal reflection.

My hope is that our shared reflection on *Amoris laetitia* and our efforts to make its teachings alive in marriages and families will bring us to a true sense of belonging to God's family as members of the household of God, as we find movingly expressed in the Letter to the Ephesians:

> **So then you are no longer strangers and aliens, but you are citizens with the saints and also members of the household of God, built**

---

1. See, for example, Louis J. Cameli, *Church, Faith, Future: What We Face, What We Can Do* (Collegeville, MN: The Liturgical Press, 2017).

upon the foundation of the apostles and prophets, with Christ Jesus himself as the cornerstone. In him the whole structure is joined together and grows into a holy temple in the Lord; in whom you also are built together spiritually into a dwelling place for God. (Ephesians 2:19–22)

☀ Questions for Reflection

1. What are the social and cultural situations that challenge families today?

2. How can the Church support families dealing with shifts in culture?

2

An Annotated Outline of *Amoris laetitia*

The Church's way, from the time of the Council of Jerusalem, has always been the way of Jesus, the way of mercy and reinstatement.

—Amoris laetitia, 296

As a formational document, *Amoris laetitia* fosters prayer, growth in discipleship on the journey of faith, and a transformation of life. The goal of formation is an ongoing conversion of heart that leads to a complete conversion of heart. If we look at the various parts of the exhortation in this light, we can begin to understand how it serves as a document on formation.

The outline that follows provides the chapter titles of *Amoris laetitia*, brief descriptions of their content, and summaries of some of the more salient sections and subsections.

CHAPTER 1: In the Light of the Word.

The opening context for considering love in the family is the Word of God. Before we begin to gather our experiences, and prior to thinking about marriage and family, we listen. God has something to say to us. Receiving the Word of God, who comes to us as Jesus Christ and as his Word in Sacred Scripture, forms the Church and forms those who are incorporated in the Church. Pope Benedict XVI says in his apostolic exhortation *Verbum Domini*: "To receive the Word means to let oneself be shaped by him and thus to be conformed by the power of the

Holy Spirit to Christ. . . . As St. Augustine puts it . . . 'You were created through the word, but now through the word you must be recreated'" (50). This opening orientation to God's formative Word becomes a regular refrain throughout *Amoris laetitia*.

CHAPTER 2: The Experiences and Challenges of Families.

The process of Christian formation takes people as they are. It meets them in their experience with its lights and shadows, its positive elements and its brokenness. It does not begin by imposing an ideal. That would disregard freedom. Christian formation begins with an honest gathering of experience and builds from there.

CHAPTER 3: Looking to Jesus; The Vocation of the Family.

Every formation process is about vocation, the unique calling that we each have. Here, that call is verified in marriage and family life. We begin with our experience, but we do not stay there. We look to Jesus, and he looks on us. In that encounter, he moves us—in our marriages and our families—beyond our experience as he draws us to himself and into the very life of God as a communion of persons.

CHAPTER 4: Love in Marriage.

To encourage a path of fidelity and mutual self-giving, the growth, strengthening, and deepening of conjugal and family love needs to be encouraged. This chapter covers:

A. **Our daily love.** Formation brings together both understanding and practical application. It is never a purely theoretical or speculative exercise. We are formed to live out a practical love in the context of the closest relationships of our lives. St. Paul's hymn to love (1 Corinthians 3:4–7) describes what love is and how it is lived.

B. **Growing in conjugal love.** Formation is a dynamic process that involves organic growth. Different dimensions of love build on each other. Sometimes this process is gradual, and sometimes it is accelerated. The following dimensions of love are highlighted:

- **LIFELONG SHARING.** Conjugal love is definitive. In other words, it is not a stage of life. It is a lifelong project just as discipleship is.

- **JOY AND BEAUTY.** Both joy and beauty in the relationship must be cultivated. A practiced and deliberate kind of noticing is essential, and it is learned.

- **MARRYING FOR LOVE.** Love moves beyond a set of feelings and attractions (as important as they might be) to a more deliberate realm of real commitment. As people approach marriage they learn to decide and so learn to commit themselves to each other.

- **A LOVE THAT REVEALS ITSELF AND INCREASES.** Married love grows. That growth occurs through the daily interactions of life and a path of learning, over and over again, how to love.

- **DIALOGUE.** "Dialogue is essential for experiencing, expressing, and fostering love in marriage and family life. Yet it can only be the fruit of a long and demanding apprenticeship" (136). The spouses form each other in the practice of dialogue by being in dialogue.

C. **Passionate love.** To symbolize the union of the human heart with God, love includes passion. The consideration of love includes:

- **THE WORLD OF EMOTIONS.** This world includes desires, feelings, and emotions. They are the passions. They can be neutral in themselves, but we must learn how they can lead us to proper action. We learn what to do with them.

- **THE EROTIC DIMENSION OF LOVE.** The sexual and erotic dimensions of the marriage relationship are integrated in a larger framework of communication and spontaneity. These dimensions are more and more clearly seen as a gift from God.

- **VIOLENCE AND MANIPULATION.** Every good gift carries the potential for deformation. And so, human sexuality in marriage can be deformed. Married couples need to learn how to move beyond "using" or "discarding" each other. This means they must move beyond any violence, forced submission, or whatever would make their relationship less human.

- **MARRIAGE AND VIRGINITY.** These different ways of life can learn from each other. They both have a common direction in loving others, but they live this out in different ways.

D. **The transformation of love.** The longevity of relationships calls for regular renewal and the reaffirmation of earlier decisions.

CHAPTER 5: Love Made Fruitful.

Life comes with love.

A. **Welcoming a new life.** Children are not just born but welcomed in gratitude and wonder. In this, we find a mirror of divine love. This section considers:

- **LOVE AND PREGNANCY.** Pregnancy is collaboration with God's creative power. Human and divine love converge: each child is loved by God and is to be loved by parents.

- **THE LOVE OF A MOTHER AND OF A FATHER.** Both parents come to terms with their unique and necessary contributions to the formation of their child.

B. **An expanding fruitfulness.** A married couple comes to recognize that their union is generative. This generativity generally means the physical generation of children, but it can also take other forms. In any case, the couple needs to commit themselves to the generativity that belongs to their relationship.

- **DISCERNING THE BODY.** The experience of the Eucharist demands that the family live it out and discern its implications, especially in terms of opening the doors of the family to those in need.

C. Life in the wider family. This is the extended family that can move us beyond any form of isolating individualism. The following are reflected upon:

- **BEING SONS AND DAUGHTERS.** Each of us is a son or daughter, and so we remain. Marriage challenges couples to find new ways of being sons and daughters.

- **THE ELDERLY.** They form families by drawing people into the continuity of generations and holding historical memory.

- **BEING BROTHERS AND SISTERS.** We are not just born as siblings, but we must also learn and be formed into deliberate and intentional ways of being brothers and sisters.

- **A BIG HEART.** The extended family can sustain and supplement the deficiencies of a nuclear family. It forms the family in a wider horizon.

CHAPTER 6: Some Pastoral Perspectives.

These are some pastoral and formational challenges.

A. Proclaiming the Gospel of the family today. Families themselves are the principal agents of the family apostolate, especially in their lived experience as domestic churches. They should be able to find a supportive matrix for their mission in the parish, which is a family of families.

B. Preparing engaged couples for marriage. This critical moment of formation depends on the entire community. The model for it can be found in the ministry of Christian initiation (known as the Rite of Christian Initiation of Adults). Preparation helps a couple to get to know each other and to prepare for their life together. At the same time, preparation also means a reproposal of the Gospel, so that a couple can go forward together in faith. The focus of preparation cannot fall exclusively on the ritual celebration of the wedding but must move forward and encompass formation for the life of the marriage that follows.

C. **Accompanying the first years of married life.** A couple needs to embrace their life as a journey and process of growth together. Their marriage is a kind of "salvation history." The couple keeps forming each other at every stage. Pastoral accompaniment is foundational. This means encouraging contact with the Word of God and fostering, in whatever way possible, growth in faith. Parishes, movements, and other institutions can be of help.

D. **Casting light on crises, worries, and difficulties.**

- **THE CHALLENGE OF CRISES.** The key to addressing the inevitable crises in families and marriages is to face them together with good communication and a steady willingness to reconcile.

- **OLD WOUNDS.** A great formational challenge within marriage is to deal with stunted early development and any prior emotional traumas that can later play out in the marriage relationship.

- **ACCOMPANIMENT AFTER BREAKDOWN AND DIVORCE.** Special pastoral accompaniment is necessary for these situations, an accompaniment that always seeks to keep people close to the believing community. Above all, the good of the children must be maintained in these difficult situations.

- **CERTAIN COMPLEX SITUATIONS.** These might include the marriage of a Catholic with a non-Catholic Christian or a non-Christian, families with persons who have a homosexual orientation, and single parents. All these situations deserve careful pastoral attention.

E. **When death makes us feel its sting.** Inevitable loss presents another shaping and formational moment for the faith of married people and families.

CHAPTER 7: Towards a Better Education of Children.

Parents need to consciously and enthusiastically carry out their role to educate and form their children.

A. **Where are our children?** Parents are formators of their children and need to understand where their children really are on their journey.

B. **The ethical formation of children.** The foundation of moral formation for children is the trust they have in their parents. This formation moves forward through dialogue and fostering good habits.

C. **The value of correction as an incentive.** Formation must include an understanding of the consequences of behavior and the need to ask for forgiveness.

D. **Patient realism.** The formation of children must recognize that they have real freedom, but that it is not absolute. Their freedom is limited and conditioned. Those responsible for their formation help them in that context.

E. **Family life as an educational setting.** The larger culture of electronic media presents a formidable challenge for the formation of children. The family remains the primary setting for that formation in the context of personal encounter, not just virtual connections.

F. **The need for sex education.** Fundamentally, this is formation for loving and self-giving. It happens through self-knowledge and through freedom from self-centeredness.

G. **Passing on faith.** Parents can only pass on faith when they trust God and are firm in their faith.

CHAPTER 8: Accompanying, Discerning, and Integrating Weakness.

Any formational accompaniment in the context of weakness and even sinfulness assumes that God's grace can be active even in weakness and frailty.

A. **Gradualness in pastoral care.** In the process of pastoral accompaniment and formation, it is essential to note in line with Pope John Paul II the law of gradualness—that is, the individual "knows, loves, and accomplishes moral good by different stages of growth" (*Familiaris consortio*, 34).

B. **The discernment of "irregular" situations.** Discernment and formation in irregular situations must, above all, take into account the particular circumstances of each person. This ministry portrays the mercy of God, which has no limitations. It assumes humility, discretion, and love for the Church and her teaching, in a sincere search for God's will and a desire to make a more perfect response to it.

C. **Mitigating factors in pastoral discernment.** In difficult and irregular situations, people may have a theoretical understanding of what is right and good but not be able to see the value for themselves and in their situation. This should be taken into account when accompanying others in irregular situations. It is also important to distinguish judgment about the objective situation from the subjective culpability of a person. In all of this, discernment and formation must always remain open to new stages of growth and to new decisions that can enable the ideal to be more fully realized.

D. **Rules and discernment.** Rules are important but insufficient in the realm of more particular circumstances. Discernment is a formative process that helps to find possible ways of responding to God in the particular circumstances of life and of growing in the midst of limits.

E. The logic of pastoral mercy. Without detracting from the ideal, pastoral formation and discernment must be set in the context of God's merciful love that is ever ready to understand, forgive, accompany, and—above all—integrate those who have fallen short of the ideal.

CHAPTER 9: The Spirituality of Marriage and the Family.

Charity, or love, is at the heart of the Christian spiritual journey, but this unfolds as a specific spirituality in family life and its relationships.

A. A spirituality of supernatural communion. A positive experience of family communion is a true path to daily sanctification and mystical growth, a means for deeper union with God.

B. Gathered in prayer in the light of Easter. A family will grow as it continues to unite itself to the Paschal Mystery of the Lord. This happens through prayer, devotion, and especially the Eucharist.

C. A spirituality of exclusive and free love. The formative love of marriage is exclusive because it is centered in faithful love to the other. At the same time, this love is freeing because it enables the partners to fully become themselves.

D. A spirituality of care, consolation, and incentive. The family that is forming itself in love will be ever more open to welcome and engage others, especially those most in need.

※ Questions for Reflection

1. From this outline, do you see any new perspectives flowing from *Amoris laetitia*?

2. What perspectives do you see as especially valuable?

3. What perspectives in *Amoris laetitia* do you wish to consider further?

3

Amoris laetitia as a Formation Document

> Married life is a process of growth, in which each spouse is God's means of helping the other to mature.
>
> —*Amoris laetitia, 221*

The Perspective of Formation

A quick review of the annotated outline of *Amoris laetitia* demonstrates the major formational themes that the exhortation encompasses. In its entirety *Amoris laetitia* is a formation document. That makes *Amoris laetitia* remarkable in the tradition of magisterial teaching. Unlike other magisterial documents, it is not about doctrine (for example, *Mystici corporis* or *Humani generis*), not about morality (for example, *Humanae vitae* or *Veritatis splendor*), not specifically about a pastoral vision (such as the continental synods in preparation for the Great Jubilee—for example, *Ecclesia in America*), and not about devotional life in the Church (for example, *Marialis cultus*). In the tradition of magisterial teaching, this exhortation represents something quite new. *Amoris laetitia* assumes and incorporates teaching on doctrine, morality, pastoral questions, and even devotional life but focuses primarily on formation. This focus has its roots in the Second Vatican Council's concern for human experience and for the journey of the pilgrim People of God.

Amoris laetitia takes real life concerns and experiences and situates marriage and family life as a focal point for conversion and transformation in the Christian life. The exhortation helps people to grow as disciples of Jesus Christ in their marriages and family life. This approach is a logical consequence of the spiritual revolution begun by St. Thérèse of Lisieux. She gave foundations for democratizing holiness. In other words, she demonstrated an immediate and full access to holiness for all people in the ordinary circumstances of their lives, and not just for an elite few.[1] Her spiritual revolution continues with this exhortation. *Amoris laetitia* engages and encourages those who are married and in family life and who are on the way to the perfection, or full actuation, of their love.

As we read *Amoris laetitia* with a "formational lens," we can detect four drivers in its composition and development that move from experience to experience transformed. The first driver is for married people and families to claim their experience with all its lights and shadows. The second is to see their experience in the light of the Gospel. The third is to hear a call to conversion. Finally, the fourth is to carry that transformed experience to a world deeply in need.

The deep roots for *Amoris laetitia* as a formation document rest in the Second Vatican Council, more specifically, in at least three important proposals of the Council: the universal call to holiness, the importance of dialogue in an *ecclesia discens et docens* (a learning and teaching church), and the journey or process dimension of the Christian life for individuals and the entire community as the pilgrim people of God.[2]

Pastors and theologians are not accustomed to a magisterial document that is formational, especially in the context of marriage and family life. Yet if they do not have this formational sense of the exhortation, they will be missing an essential hermeneutical or interpretative key for a correct understanding and application of *Amoris laetitia*.

---

1. See her description of "the little way" in *Story of a Soul: The Autobiography of St. Thérèse of Lisieux*, trans. John Clarke, 2nd ed. (Washington, DC: ICS Publications, 1976), p. 188.
2. See *Ecclesiam suam*, especially 78–83 (1964); *Lumen gentium*, chapters 5 and 7.

Controversies and debates surrounding *Amoris laetitia* have their source in a lack of understanding of the nature of the document as formational. As noted earlier, prior theological and magisterial developments for marriage and family dealt with juridical questions and the one theological question of the sacramentality of marriage. They then expanded to include questions of rights and morality.

Amoris laetitia assumes established doctrine, moral teaching, and law concerning marriage and family life. There are no changes, despite claims to the contrary in some quarters. The exhortation, however, offers spiritual and moral formation by helping people to live out and grow in their commitment to Jesus as disciples who are married and in family life. The exhortation assumes that the Christian life unfolds in a process. It also assumes that Christian life has ideals that remain even when we fail to reach them. Finally, it assumes that neither programs nor pronouncements, but only God's grace, leads us forward, although we can create—with God's help—those favorable conditions for accepting that grace. All this confirms the unique character of *Amoris laetitia* as a magisterial document of formation.

Formation in this context never means stamping out Christians in cookie-cutter fashion. It does mean attention to the concrete and particular, the unique and unrepeatable story of this individual, this marriage, and this family.

Particular Elements of Formation

For some, the notion of formation remains vague. In fact, *Amoris laetitia* envisions clear and precise elements of Christian formation. Consider, for example, the following six elements.

1. Immersion in the Word of God. Our formation and transformation depends, first of all, on God's communication to us, his revelation, and his invitation to share life with him. "By this revelation, then, the invisible God, from the fullness of his love, addresses men [and women] as his friends, and moves among them, in order to invite and receive them into his own company."[3] *Amoris laetitia* begins with a meditation on the Word of God contained in Sacred Scripture and then, at every important juncture of its development, returns to that Word.

2. A reading of human experience. Genuine ministry to the formation of disciples of Jesus begins as Jesus did—with their experience. It starts with the ordinary experiences of life. Jesus began with the hurting, the distressed, those deemed unsuccessful by the world's standards, and, of course, sinners. Their experiences included all the lights and the shadows of their lives.

Beginning with human experience does not mean staying enclosed in that experience. Human experiences are drawn in and up into the mystery of God, who works through Jesus Christ in the power of the Holy Spirit and then entirely transforms human experience.

3. A sense of journey. One of the great treasures of the Second Vatican Council was the recovery of the dynamism of the Christian life. The unfolding and development of tradition, for example, *Dei verbum* (the *Constitution on Divine Revelation*), gives a sense of how the Church grows across time in a greater appreciation and understanding of the mysteries of faith. The image of the pilgrim People of God in *Lumen gentium* (chapter 7) reinserted the Church in history and described the journey that we make together. In spiritual formation, that same dynamism and sense of process plays a decisive role. *Amoris laetitia* sees married couples and their families in movement on a journey of unfolding grace. Note, however, that this journey of marriage and family life does not always move in a straight line. Our lives and our understanding are limited. Sometimes, we sin and fail to live out the ideal in God's plan. Still, when couples and families commit themselves to the journey, God's grace will assuredly lead them home. Along the way, they will experience growth and development in their faith, hope, and love.

---

3. *Dei verbum*, 2.

4. The help of accompaniment, discernment, and integration.
We cannot form or transform ourselves, and we cannot do that for others. We can, however, accept and extend help so that we and others can be more open to receive the formation and transformation that God offers in the power of the Holy Spirit. Three forms of help—accompaniment, discernment, and integration—figure prominently in *Amoris laetitia*. They foster the journey of unfolding and development that belongs to the pilgrim People of God in their individual and collective journeys, including those of married couples and families. Accompaniment is the faithful presence that a believer extends to others. It means reminding others of the presence and action of God and being a voice of encouragement and challenge as people face inevitable struggles on the journey. Discernment is the practice of attention and watchfulness that is attuned to the direction that God may be giving to an individual or community. Discernment does not so much figure things out as watch for the emergence of God's truth in our lived situations. Integration means connecting our individual lives and experiences to the larger flow of the Church's life. Integration fosters the sense of belonging, which, in turn, supports and encourages perseverance in our commitments.

5. Facing challenges. Spiritual formation certainly involves embracing ideals and trying to live them out. The call of Jesus in the Gospel invites us to full-hearted commitment, and that often includes significant sacrifice. At the same time, spiritual formation must be unafraid to face complex situations that sometimes veer away from the ideal. It is not a matter of surrendering to what is less than ideal but rather facing the real situation and moving forward as best as one can. We can only face challenges in the measure that we have confidence that God walks with us patiently encouraging and helping us to live out our commitments, even in less than ideal circumstances. In chapter 8, when *Amoris laetitia* deals with "irregular" situations, it is unflinching in facing difficulties. All this belongs to formation in an integral sense.

6. Realistic hope. Formation attends to the here and now, and at the same time, it looks beyond the present moment and anticipates that God is drawing us into the fullness of life. That is our destiny and our hope, and it rests in God's promise that Jesus offers us. *Amoris laetitia* is suffused with this kind of realistic hope and so provides a viable horizon for spiritual formation for marriages and families. From its beginning, the exhortation notes the challenges that beset marriage and family life in today's world. It also notes the challenging and sometimes "irregular" situations of Christians trying to live out their commitments. At every juncture, however, *Amoris laetitia* offers the hope and promise of the Gospel to draw people forward and to keep them encouraged on the journey.

Although not exhaustive, this list of six elements demonstrates how the exhortation is a formational document whose aim is to promote the spiritual formation of married couples and families.

Those Who Serve the Formation of Married Couples and Families

Both priests and laity play a role in the formation of married couples and families. *Amoris laetitia* states that families are on the frontlines as agents of formation for other families. Those who serve marriage and family formation, whether clergy or laity, share common tasks. The following are ten actions that belong to those ministering to marriages and families.

1. Summoning and proclaiming. Formators must, first of all, summon the community to be attentive to a direction that God is giving them. In this context, they proclaim a particular word, which is the "Gospel of the family." This is the Good News that the saving power of Jesus Christ and his Holy Spirit takes hold of people in the most intimate relationships of their lives, in marriage and family life. In these circumstances, often beset with difficulties, challenges, and sometimes sin, God in Jesus Christ offers hope and healing. People can come to the fullness of love and life in God in their journey of marriage and family life. That is Good News. And it must first be proclaimed.

2. Repeating the summons and call. Because marriage and family life is a journey, circumstances change, sometimes in positive directions and sometimes more negatively. In any case, it is insufficient to call people once and then move on. Formators must regularly repeat the summons and the proclamation. In new circumstances, the Gospel of the family will take on a different appearance and new meaning. In *Amoris laetitia*, Pope Francis follows a spiral development. He returns periodically to foundational themes of marriage and family life, as he circles around them. Similarly, family formators need to return to foundational realities and invitations.

3. Accompanying. Accompanying people means being actively and faithfully present to them. It also means serving as a voice of reassurance, challenge, and encouragement. Although initially accompaniment may not seem to be of great significance, it is important. Accompaniment is a kind of sacramental representation of God's presence to his people. God faithfully walks with his people, even when they are unaware of his presence among them. The formator who accompanies people on their spiritual journey serves as an effective sign of the presence of God. In this way, accompaniment points to the ultimate source of reassurance for those on the journey. The presence of a minister who represents the presence of God offers an anchor in an otherwise turbulent sea.

4. Letting go. It may seem paradoxical to claim "letting go" as a task of formation, but it is. Once one has done all that can be done, to let go is to trust the freedom of others and the action of God's grace. Letting go respects the adult faith of others. For example, in *Amoris laetitia*, Pope Francis says that we are called to form people's consciences and not to replace them (37). No one can foster the formation and growth of another unless that person respects and trusts that grace is at work. This means respect for the freedom and autonomy of others.

Letting go is the exact opposite of a controlling mindset, so often rooted in a misplaced sense of responsibility for others. Letting go is an act of faith and trust in God, who is the one who moves and transforms lives.

5. Inviting dialogue. Formators invite dialogue and engage in it. In this process of listening and speaking, they enable those they serve to see and assess their experience and, from that, to begin to chart the path of greater commitment to the Lord. The entire process that culminated in the composition of *Amoris laetitia* was itself a grand dialogue. The first synod on the family (2014) sought to identify the contemporary challenges to marriage and family life. The raw material for that synod was gleaned from a worldwide dialogue of bishops with their people. There was listening and then a synthesis of results that was brought to the synod in Rome. Similarly, the second synod on the family (2015) sought to offer helpful responses to the questions and concerns that had been generated the year before. Again, a worldwide process of listening created a basic text for the synod meeting. In addition to this dialogue at the local level with spouses and families, the synods themselves deliberately embraced synodality, that is, a collegial process of honest sharing and creative collaboration. Moving forward, then, means that family and marriage formation must continually engage in the same process of dialogue.

6. Simultaneously teaching and learning. If formation is rooted in true dialogue, it moves in different directions. Those who bring formation to others certainly teach, but they also learn from those they teach. Similarly, those who are served will learn, but they will also teach. This pattern reflects the reality of the Church itself as *ecclesia discens et docens*, a church that both teaches and learns. The two synods on the family are models for this double modality. The Church learns from those who belong to it, in this case, from married couples and families. The Church also learns from the world, as Pope Paul VI affirmed in his encyclical *Ecclesiam suam* (1964). Most importantly, the Church learns from the promptings of the Holy Spirit, whom Jesus promised and who leads us into "all truth" (John 16:13). At the same time, the Church teaches those who belong to her and teaches the world itself. Formation in this learning-teaching process can only occur when there is docility, that quality the spiritual tradition describes as "teachableness" grounded in humility. Overall, formators and those in formation need to be open to change and to be changed.

7. Holding the vision. Circumstances change, and people change as well. Through all the change, however, there is a stable point fixed in the larger vision. For example, for marriage and family life, there is a history of change, and even today there is a wide variety of experiences based on the diversity of cultures. In the context of formation, an overarching vision holds these experiences together. Regularly in *Amoris laetitia*, Pope Francis alludes to love in marriage and family life as a reflection of and a participation in Trinitarian communion, the love and union of the Father, Son, and Holy Spirit. Inside the changes and the diversity, there is a unifying vision of who we are becoming. That vision is divine love and communion. That is the destination toward which we are now partially, imperfectly, and yet assuredly tending. It is essential for formators of families and marriages to hold that vision up for all to see, just as Pope Francis does.

8. Counting the gifts. To help people correct their direction, formators may sometimes need to cite failures to live up to an ideal. More importantly, they need to name the gifts and the graces that are already a part of the lives of the individuals they are accompanying. As the gifts are embraced, they provide people an incentive to move forward. This formative pattern is evident in St. Paul's writings. Biblical commentators speak of the Pauline indicative and the Pauline imperative. In other words, Paul first points to what is given (the indicative) and then, as a consequence, says what is to be done (the imperative). "So if you have been raised with Christ, seek the things that are above, where Christ is, seated at the right hand of God" (Colossians 3:1). Similarly in *Amoris laetitia*, Pope Francis emphasizes the blessings and the gifts of marriage and family life. Those gifts are a formative gateway to action and change. Anyone who wants to foster marriage and family life must be attuned to the gifts that are already at work in the lives of people and be willing to articulate them and share them.

9. Focusing on individuals. Catholics share a common formation, especially through the liturgy, which enables us to enter the mystery of the dying and rising of the Lord together. The liturgical year recreates our shared salvation history. This common formation embodies the Lord's action in forming a people for himself. As essential as this shared experience is, it does not exhaust the formational process. In addition to the shared elements of our vocation, we are summoned by name to share new life with the Lord and each other. Very often in *Amoris laetitia*, Pope Francis indicates the individual and particular dimension of formation for marriage and family life. He invites anyone engaged in formation to be respectful of differences and particular circumstances. This is especially important when family and marriage situations are complex and perhaps troubled. Rote formulas, he often insists, are inadequate. Those engaged in formation must have this awareness as they go forward. At the same time, individual and particular circumstances do not leave people isolated and disconnected. Focusing on individuals also means integrating them into the larger community.

10. Watching and discerning. Those who serve the formation of marriages and families have a fundamental and critical responsibility to keep watch with the people they serve. Together, they are attentive to God's movements and directions. This is discernment, as we considered it earlier. It is not a matter of applying our powers of intellect and figuring things out. It is rather a waiting and watching that leads to the discovery of where God is leading us in our particular circumstances. Discernment is an irreplaceable service of formation that goes beyond generalities and helps people to make sense of their experience and how God is summoning them in the moment.

☀ Questions for Reflection

1. How do you understand formation in the faith?

2. How do you see formation as part of the spiritual life of all disciples?

3. How does formation apply to ministry to married couples and families?

4

The Challenges to Spiritual-Moral Formation

Many people feel that the Church's message on marriage and the family does not clearly reflect the preaching and attitudes of Jesus, who set forth a demanding ideal yet never failed to show compassion and closeness to the frailty of individuals like the Samaritan woman or the woman caught in adultery.

—Amoris laetitia, 38

Amoris laetitia envisions spiritual-moral formation as a process that helps marriages and families who make the Christian journey. This formation may not be easy, but it certainly is not impossible. To consider this formational process in more detail, it will be helpful to identify the challenges that formators and families face as they make their way.

In the following section, we will consider three kinds of challenges: (1) external challenges that stem primarily from the culture in which we live; (2) challenges that are internal to the life of the Church and that summon us to what Pope Francis has called "pastoral conversion"; (3) finally, *Amoris laetitia* identifies a number of particular formational challenges for marriage and family life.

External Challenges

The external challenges to formation stem mainly from our culture. The Canadian philosopher Charles Taylor, in *A Secular Age*[1], has examined our current North American cultural situation from a philosophical and historical perspective. He helps us to understand that we live in a secular age that has been in development for some five centuries. In it, emphasis falls on the *saeculum*, this world and its autonomy. There is, as the Second Vatican Council indicated, a healthy form of secularity that gives a rightful autonomy to the things of this world.[2] The secularity that Taylor describes and that we live in differs from that. Our secular age insists on a rightful autonomy of the things of the world, but it does so in a way that excludes any reference to God or transcendent purpose. The prevalent secularity is associated with a radical immanentism—in other words, an assertion that there is no reference point outside of this world and life as we now know it. With that assertion, there are significant consequences for human behavior and decisions. If I really only have my world and myself, then that is the full measure of my life. That measure means a subjective and relative standard for establishing values and making decisions. When everything is relative, there is consequently no objective morality, nor is there a standard independent of my experience by which I could measure and evaluate my experience.

Taylor also identifies another shaping feature of our secular age. He notes a fundamental vision of life proposed by Jean-Jacques Rousseau that marks the worldview of so many of our contemporaries. Rousseau was convinced that nature, including human nature, was absolutely good. The corollary of this was the denial, at a fundamental level, of sin, brokenness, and division as part of the human condition. If Rousseau's position is true, there is no need for redemption and no need for individuals and communities to embark on a journey of forgiveness, healing, and restoration.

---

1. Charles Taylor, *A Secular Age* (Cambridge, MA: Harvard University Press, 2007).
2. See *Gaudium et spes*, "Rightful Autonomy of Earthly Affairs," 36.

A third marker of our secular age is the commercialization of all interactions, with its consequent impact on human relationships. This means that our overall response to life in our secular age is a measured and economic response. Obviously, if this world and this life are all that we have, we will carefully make our way ever mindful of cost and benefit to us. This perspective is very narrow.

There are other pieces to Taylor's detailed analysis of our secular age, but these capture the heart of the matter. Taken altogether, these elements give us a picture of a closed-end secularity, a kind of law unto itself. Unlike the secularity proposed by the Second Vatican Council that envisions a rightful autonomy of earthly affairs in conjunction with a sense of ultimate dependence on God, our secular age narrows down the range of life and options to this world. The consequences are far-reaching. Moral and ethical life is deeply impacted. The net effect, in the words of Christian Smith, who has studied the moral and spiritual life of young people, is "morality adrift." This crystallizes the formidable external challenge to spiritual-moral formation in our time and in our culture. We can consider this in more detail.

Christian Smith is a professor of sociology and director of the Center for the Study of Religion and Society at the University of Notre Dame. Over the years, he has followed a group of young people through adolescence and into young adulthood. This represents the next generation to marry and start families, if they so decide. Smith has observed these young people through the prism of faith, spirituality, and morality. His latest study is entitled *Lost in Transition: The Dark Side of Emerging Adulthood*.[3] The book yields a troubling picture of the young people he studies. They seem to lack four essential formative ingredients that would enable them to move forward with their spiritual-moral lives in positive and constructive ways. They lack (1) a moral framework for their lives, (2) a vocabulary or language to express moral questions and directions, (3) tools for moral reasoning, and (4) an

---

3. Christian Smith et al., *Lost in Transition: The Dark Side of Emerging Adulthood* (New York: Oxford University Press, 2011).

A New Vision of Family Life

explicit sense of higher purpose or transcendence. These young people, who are moving toward marriage and family life, represent a stark formational challenge for those who want to minister to them.

Two questions arise from this troubling situation: How did we arrive at this point? Is there anything we can do to break out of this moral-spiritual desert? Some writers have attempted to offer a historical analysis to explain our current situation. For example, James Davison Hunter has traced the history of moral education in the United States.[4] As important as the historical question is, the more urgent question for those in pastoral ministry is how we can constructively address the challenges to spiritual and moral formation with an eye on the future of marriage and family life.

Charles Taylor persuasively argues that we cannot reverse the process of secularization that is deeply entrenched in our culture and that gives rise to these spiritual and moral dilemmas. There are, however, ways to address the formational challenges in today's context that draw from strategies rooted in the Word of God.

Two elements found in the Word of God make for compelling and effective moral-spiritual formation and transformation. They are *narrative and connection* or, expressed differently, *story and relationship*.

The story is not just any story. Nor is it a moralizing parable. The fundamental story is the story of God's involvement with humanity. This means a joint narrative of God and his creation. What emerges from this intertwined story of God and humanity is our connection and relationship with God, most particularly in the Christian tradition, our relationship in Jesus Christ by the power of the Holy Spirit. Narrative and connection or story and relationship—these are the compelling and effective foundations of moral formation and transformation. Consider two biblical passages, one from the Old Testament and one from the New Testament.

---

4. James Davison Hunter, *The Death of Character: Moral Education in an Age without Good or Evil* (New York: Basic Books, 2000).

We read in the Book of Exodus 20:2: "I am the LORD your God, who brought you out of the land of Egypt, out of the house of slavery; you shall have no other gods before me." Then follow the other nine commandments while dwelling on the verse. Though brief, the verse is also essential for the entire moral vision embodied in the Commandments.

This verse speaks of a story of grace and liberation. God takes initiative and frees his people from the slavery of Egypt. The narrative of this liberation belongs both to God and to the people of Israel. It is an intertwined narrative, and out of it is born an entirely unique connection, or relationship, between God and his people. "I am the LORD your God." In light of that story and that relationship, the Commandments make sense as a life direction.

The same pattern is evident in the New Testament, for example, in this passage from St. Paul: "It is no longer I who live, but it is Christ who lives in me. And the life I now live in the flesh I live by faith in the Son of God who loved me and gave himself for me" (Galatians 2:20). Notice the elements of story and relationship. Paul identifies the core story of Jesus, the Son of God, who out of love gave up his life on the Cross for us. What emerges from that story is a relationship and connection of unsurpassed intimacy: "It is no longer I who live, but it is Christ who lives in me."

The conjunction of narrative and relationship is at the heart of marriage and family life as *Amoris laetitia* presents it. This means that genuine existence—in the narrative and in the relationship—is already of itself formative and transformative. All this certainly does not easily resolve the external challenges for spiritual and moral formation posed by our secular age, but it marks a beginning for understanding and action.

Challenges Internal to the Life of the Church

Spiritual-moral formation is essential to the ministry of the Church. Many assume that the plan for formation is clear and only needs to be applied. In fact, it is more complicated. Mindsets and perspectives in the internal life of the Church can impede and even block the process of moral-spiritual formation. Sometimes this stems from history and sometimes from an imperfect grasp of what God desires from us. The following are six challenges to spiritual-moral formation that belong to the internal life of the Church. Later, we can explore how to confront those challenges and turn them around with a pastoral conversion to which Pope Francis tirelessly summons the Church.

1. Residual Jansenism. At the heart of Jansenism, a tendency in doctrine and piety that began in the seventeenth century, is a dark understanding of human nature under the dominion of sin. It also embodied a moral rigorism that is clearly at variance with Jesus' message of mercy. For example, Jansenism might propose that if one were in the state of serious sin, that person could do no good work, and no actual grace could be active in that person. These and similar propositions were condemned by Pope Clement XI.[5] The essential problem and error of Jansenism is that it binds grace and restricts how God can move and act. Although Jansenism was condemned by the Church, and some authors suggest that this heresy was resolved by the beginning of the nineteenth century, its effects have lingered. This is evident when people, even today, assert the preeminence of law over love and declare that divine justice must prevail over divine mercy, as if the two were in competition. The distortion introduced by these Jansenistic tendencies obviously creates a challenge for a proper spiritual-moral formation that must always affirm the primacy of grace and love.

2. Legalism. The mindset of legalism understands the moral-spiritual life mainly as the application of law to given situations or decisions. This approach reduces the spiritual-moral life to the technical application of rules. Of course, values, norms, and laws have an entirely valid and necessary place in orienting the moral life of Christians. The problem is reducing the whole of the moral life to their technical application. Doing so binds human freedom and makes it superfluous.

---

5. See his constitution *Unigenitus Dei Filius* (September 8, 1713) "Jansenistic Errors of Pasquier Quesnel," in Denzinger, 43rd ed., 2400–2502.

3. Idealism. A fixation on ideals is a hazard for those who want to follow an intentional Christian path. They are rightly drawn to the high and demanding ideals of the Gospel that Jesus proclaimed and that the Church teaches. If, however, they become fixed exclusively on the ideal, the spiritual life becomes a matter of "all or nothing." Idealism, then, becomes an enemy of realism. It becomes difficult, if not impossible, to accept the path of patient travel that encompasses struggles and failures while on the way toward embracing the full ideal.

4. An ahistorical mentality. Some people cannot accept that they are in history, on a journey, and part of a process. They deny the individual and collective journey that is part of the Christian life. For them, only two things matter: the state of sin and the state of grace. In fact, a state of sin exists in which we are alienated from God and others. Also existing is a state of grace in which we share the life of the indwelling Trinity. To focus narrowly and exclusively on these states is, by definition, to claim a static approach to the Christian life. In fact, there is a dynamism in living out the life of discipleship. That dynamism entails a movement that can have complications and less than ideal twists and turns. Only in the acceptance of our pilgrim status and provisional existence can we go forward with the humble recognition that we have not yet arrived and we will not arrive this side of death. With the acceptance of the journey and ourselves as pilgrims, we can be more pliable and ready to experience spiritual-moral formation.

5. A lost sense of sacramental life. The sacraments foster and nourish Catholics in the Christian life, immersing them in the mystery of Christ. We are transformed by what we celebrate, and we are transformed into what we celebrate. The sacraments form us, but they are not to be reduced to the moment of their ritual celebration. The sacraments are to be celebrated and then lived. When the sense of living the sacraments is lost, emphasis falls on the ritual moment, and the formative dimension is lost. The ritual moment and the life that follows need to be integrated. For example, the celebration of the Eucharist should not only draw us into union with the Lord and each other in the ritual moment, but it should become an imperative for living in union with the Lord and others. Forgiveness in the Sacrament of Penance is not only given with the words of absolution; forgiveness is also meant to shape our daily pattern for interacting with others.

6. Impatience. Although it is not particular to the Church, impatience can take hold of communities of believers. This leads to a drive to judgment and to the drawing of conclusions, often prematurely. Although the energy inside of impatience can be a positive desire to get things done, impatience can often foreclose possibilities. Ultimately, impatience is the enemy of formation, which must necessarily follow its own timing and pacing.

As we consider these challenges to fostering spiritual moral-formation that are internal to the life of the Church, we may wonder if there is anything that can be done to address them. Each challenge poses questions and complexity, but some simple responses can be made. For residual Jansenism, let God's grace move freely, even in ways that might be surprising. For legalism, appreciate real human freedom, which is a gift of God. For idealism, be continuously grounded in the real world. For the ahistorical mentality, embrace the journey dimension of the Christian life. For the lost sense of sacramental life, realign sacramental awareness to move beyond the ritual moment and to the possibilities of living out the sacraments. For impatience, embrace the process of patient accompaniment.

To foster spiritual-moral formation, we need to know the resistances and the counterforces that pull people away from the task of formation. We began by noting some of the external challenges, primarily in the culture and in our historical moment. These external challenges focused mainly on a closed-end secularity that has a pervasive impact on our lives. It encourages individualism and relativism. It leaves little or no room for a transcendent reference point.

In the internal life of the Church, we discovered a number of challenges that were often the other face of something quite good. For example, Jansenism's positive side might be a readiness to see the sinful and broken dimensions of our human existence. Legalism's other side is the desire to be faithful to what God asks of us. Other similar examples can be made. In these instances, we can often discover elements that may begin positively but, in fact, eventually impede an effective spiritual-moral formation.

Moral-Spiritual Formation Challenges in *Amoris laetitia*

Besides the formational challenges that emerge in our culture and in the internal life of the Church, there are moral-spiritual challenges in the very text of *Amoris laetitia*. These challenges are not primarily about negative elements that need to be overcome. Rather, they are the challenges of sustaining and implementing a vision of marriage and family life rooted in the Gospel. Consider the following passages from *Amoris laetitia* and the accompanying commentary.

> We have long thought that simply by stressing doctrinal, bioethical, and moral issues, without encouraging openness to grace, we were providing sufficient support to families, strengthening the marriage bond, and giving meaning to marital life. We find it difficult to present marriage more as a dynamic path to personal development and fulfillment than as a lifelong burden. We also find it hard to make room for the consciences of the faithful, who very often respond as best they can to the Gospel amid their limitations and are capable of carrying out their own discernment in complex situations. We have been called to form consciences, not to replace them. (*Amoris laetitia*, 37)

> Marital love is not defended primarily by presenting indissolubility as a duty or by repeating doctrine, but by helping it to grow ever stronger under the impulse of grace. (*Amoris laetitia*, 134)

These two passages invite the Church and her ministers to take a step forward, as they serve spiritual formation. This does not mean that they discard doctrine, bioethics, and morality. It means that they expand the range of care to families by linking family and marriage experience with the spiritual journey. Notice how this perspective includes but also moves beyond doctrinal and moral teaching. It also stands in contrast to a more secular psychological approach that helps people to adjust and adapt to the problems and circumstances of their lives. Such formation fosters openness to grace and the impulse of grace. It reaches beyond conformity to doctrine and moral teaching to embrace a path of transformation.

A special challenge of spiritual formation is to respect the particular person, the particular relationship, and the particular journey with all its complexity. Within that, formation must encourage the freedom of persons to embrace what God wants. That is the meaning of the call "to form consciences, not to replace them."

> The grace of the sacrament of marriage is intended before all else "to perfect the couple's love" (*Catechism of the Catholic Church*, 1641). (*Amoris laetitia*, 89)

> We should not however confuse different levels: There is no need to lay upon two limited persons the tremendous burden of having to reproduce perfectly the union existing between Christ and his church, for marriage as a sign entails "a dynamic process . . . one that advances gradually with the progressive integration of the gifts of God" (*Familiaris consortio*, 9). (*Amoris laetitia*, 122)

These two passages link essential themes of spiritual formation. The first passage cites the *Catechism* and speaks of marriage as a path of perfecting love—that is, a couple's love for each other and their love of God. In effect, this affirmation envisions the lived experience of the Sacrament of Matrimony as the trajectory of the married couple's whole spiritual journey. The culmination of the spiritual life is the perfection of charity or love. That destination coincides with the horizon for a sacramental marriage. Some caution, however, is needed here. The word and concept of "perfection" often has been misunderstood. In English, "perfection" has a connotation of being finished and completed in the best way possible. In the spiritual tradition, "perfection" can also carry that sense, but only when one's life is completed on this earth. While we remain on this earthly journey, "perfection" means not completion but full actuation. This full engagement is not an achievement or a finished product but a horizon for living and acting. For that reason, the citation from paragraph 122, with its reference to Pope John Paul II's words from *Familiaris consortio*, is so important. Serving the formation of married couples and families, or anyone else for that matter, always means encouraging them along the journey to advance gradually and to integrate progressively the fullness of Christian life. Notice, too, how this understanding moves us once again beyond a narrow focus on "state of sin" or "state of grace."

> This effort calls for missionary conversion by everyone in the church, that is, one that is not content to proclaim a merely theoretical message without connection to people's real problems (see *Relatio synodi*, 2014, 32). *(Amoris laetitia, 201)*

This passage reformulates the task and responsibility for spiritual formation in the context of marriage and family life. It considers the ministry of the Church and summons the Church to a missionary conversion. To speak of a missionary conversion means that the Church is embarking on something quite new or, perhaps more accurately, something that is being newly reclaimed. There are multiple aspects to this missionary conversion. The text, however, is clear in indicating one major shift. Emphasis moves from a focus on a message to a focus on persons. The delivery of a theoretical message (which may have its own value in a given context) is insufficient for doing spiritual formation. What truly matters is personal connection with the dilemmas, challenges, and problems of daily life. And so the focus falls on the persons who are cared for.

> Change, improvement, the flowering of the good qualities present in each person—all these are possible. Each marriage is a kind of "salvation history," which from fragile beginnings—thanks to God's gift and a creative and generous response on our part—grows over time into something, precious and enduring. . . . At every new stage they can keep "forming" one another. *(Amoris laetitia, 221)*

This passage captures marriage as a spiritual journey by identifying it as "a kind of salvation history." In other words, the spiritual journey of marriage recapitulates the essential movements we have come to know from the great story of our salvation, our redemption in Jesus Christ. At the same time, in a few words the passage describes the central rhythm of the Christian life as God's offer of grace and our free response to that grace. Finally, there is an indication that spiritual formation does not just come from without; it is also internal to the family-marriage relationships: "they can keep 'forming' one another."

> **What is most important is the ability lovingly to help them grow in freedom, maturity, overall discipline, and real autonomy.**
> (*Amoris laetitia*, 261)

The general section on the education of children identifies a goal of all spiritual formation—growth in freedom. Freedom is central in the spiritual education of children. That freedom, as we know and understand it from St. Paul, is the freedom of the children of God, the freedom to be ourselves in God.[6]

The particular formational challenges that emerge directly from *Amoris laetitia* continue in a concentrated way in two chapters of the exhortation, chapter 4, "Love in Marriage," and chapter 8, "Accompanying, Discerning, and Integrating Weakness."

---

6. See, for example, Romans 8:18–28.

☀ *Questions for Reflection*

1. What challenges to the moral and spiritual life are especially formidable in our society?

2. Do you have confidence that these challenges can be met pastorally?

3. How does your faith help you confront the challenges our time presents?

5

New Horizons for Love and Formation

Marital joy can be experienced even amid sorrow; it involves accepting that marriage is an inevitable mixture of enjoyment and struggles, tensions and repose, pain and relief, satisfactions and longings, annoyances and pleasures, but always on the path of friendship, which inspires married couples to care for one another: "they help and serve each other."

—Amoris laetitia, 126

Across human history, men and women have married because they loved each other. Love, however, has not always been counted as an essential requirement for marriage. In 1920, one set of my grandparents entered into an arranged marriage. They met for the first time at a train station in Chicago after my grandmother's trans-Atlantic journey from Italy. Historically, in our Catholic tradition, the essential driver in establishing a marriage was not love but free consent. This continues in current canon law.[1] Marriage as a culmination of the romantic love of two people is not a universal or necessarily normative reality.

Obviously, love in marriage is not absent from our tradition, as it certainly was not absent for my grandparents, who came to love each other. The Letter to the Ephesians gives eloquent witness to what love

---

1. See canons 1055–1057. Canon 1057 reads: "Marriage is brought about through the consent of the parties, legitimately manifested between persons who are capable according to law of giving consent."

in a marriage can mean sacramentally: "Husbands, love your wives, just as Christ loved the church and gave himself up for her. . . . This is a great mystery, and I am applying it to Christ and the church" (Ephesians 5:25, 32). Historically, however, the teaching on marriage placed a heavy emphasis on consent and on the procreation of children as the principal good and goal of marriage.

In the twentieth century, Church teaching on marriage developed and sought to integrate the loving-unitive dimension of marriage with procreation. This development gained momentum in *Gaudium et spes* (*Pastoral Constitution on the Church in the Modern World*).[2] Then in 1968, Pope Paul VI's encyclical *Humanae vitae* further elaborated and insisted on the integration of the unitive and procreative dimensions of marriage.[3] The *Catechism of the Catholic Church*, citing *Lumen gentium*, 11, speaks of the Sacrament of Matrimony as "intended to perfect the couple's love."[4] Finally, in *Familiaris consortio*, Pope John Paul II describes conjugal love as the synthesis and grand integrator of all the essential elements of the Sacrament of Matrimony.[5] This line of development moves the love of the spouses, which may have earlier been viewed as peripheral, to the very center of sacramental life.

With this historical context, the remarkable development of *Amoris laetitia*, especially in chapter 4, becomes apparent. The teaching on love in marriage develops across time until it reaches a central position. The

---

2. See *Gaudium et spes*, 48.

3. "By means of the reciprocal personal gift of self, proper and exclusive to them, husband and wife tend toward the communion of their beings in view of mutual personal perfection, to collaborate with God in the generation and education of new lives" (*Amoris laetitia*, 8).

4. *Catechism of the Catholic Church*, 1641.

5. "Conjugal loves involves a totality, in which all the elements of the person enter—appeal of the body and instinct, power of feeling and affectivity, aspiration of the spirit and of will. It aims at a deeply personal unity, a unity that, beyond union in one flesh, leads to forming one heart and soul; it demands *indissolubility* and *faithfulness* in definitive mutual giving; and it is open to *fertility*. In a word it is a question of the normal characteristics of all natural conjugal love, but with a new significance which not only purifies and strengthens them, but raises them to the extent of making them the expression of specifically Christian values" (*Familiaris consortio*, 13).

A New Vision of Family Life

exhortation then breaks new ground by describing *how that love grows and unfolds in a marriage* and *how that love comes to perfection or full actuation in the individual spouses*, that is, their spiritual journeys. *Amoris laetitia* takes the centrality of love in marriage and then addresses it as a grace that is given and a grace that needs to be received. This formative-experiential perspective of *Amoris laetitia* clearly intends to foster growth in the Christian life by addressing the practical experiences of married couples and inviting them to conversion. This is the task of spiritual formation: identifying experience and then indicating in practical ways how that experience can be transformed through a conversion of heart.

Chapter 4, "Love in Marriage," proceeds in four parts: (1) our daily love, which is an extended reflection on Paul's hymn to love in 1 Corinthians with applications to marriage and family life; (2) growing in conjugal love, which describes the dynamism of love in marriage and family life; (3) passionate love, which considers the challenge of integrating the erotic dimension of love in marriage; (4) the transformation of love, which identifies the direction and destination of love in marriage and family life. Each part will be considered in greater detail from the perspective of spiritual formation. Before we do that, however, we need to consider love itself in the spiritual journey in its universal dimensions.

The growing and transformative love of the spouses for each other brings about the perfection of their relationship in marriage and, by extension, the relationships that belong to their family. This love, however, is not enclosed in their spousal relationship but brings them into the very love of God, which is the goal and perfection of the Christian life. St. Thomas Aquinas stated that love is the perfection of the Christian life:

> I would respond saying that each thing is said to be perfect in so far as it reaches its own goal or end, which is the ultimate perfection of a thing. Charity, however, is what unites us to God, who is the ultimate goal or end of the human spirit: because he who remains in love, remains in God and God in him, as we find in

1 John 4:16. And therefore the perfection of the Christian life is to be particularly considered according to love.[6]

Another doctor of the church, St. Thérèse of Lisieux came to understand that love is everything in the Church and, indeed, in the Christian life.[7]

The measure of Christian marriage and of the entire Christian life is love. The spiritual revolution of St. Thérèse of Lisieux reclaimed the centrality of love in the Christian life. She broke through the dominant boundaries of her religious-cultural milieu, which had, in so many ways, been shaped by Jansenistic tendencies. Her assertion of the primacy of love is a counterpoint to those who gauged the Christian life by conformity to laws, the multiplication of pious observances, or the embrace of extreme ascetical practices.

What does all this mean for chapter 4 of *Amoris laetitia*, "Love in marriage"? What, at first, might appear to be a predictable exhortation on love, in fact, pulls us in with a powerful gravitational force into the very center of the Christian life. Chapter 4 is not just advice and encouragement for couples to live harmoniously together; the chapter situates marriage and family life in the arena of Christian existence. It raises essential questions: Will we love or not love? How shall we love? Where does this love lead us?

Before a detailed examination of chapter 4, there is another piece of important background to be considered. Beside that part of the spiritual revolution of St. Thérèse of Lisieux to reclaim the primacy of love, she also promoted what we earlier called the democratization of holiness. Her "little way" meant that all people, no matter their situation

---

6. "Respondeo dicendum quod unumquodque dicitur esse perfectum inquantum attingit proprium finem, qui est ultima rei perfectio. Caritas autem est quae unit nos Deo, qui est ultimus finis humanae mentis: quia *qui manet in caritate, in Deo manet, et Deus in eo*, ut dicitur 1 Io. 4, 16. Et ideo secundum caritatem specialiter attenditur perfectio vitae christianae" (*Summa theologiae* II–II, q. 184, a. 1).

7. So she writes: "And the Apostle explains how all the most perfect gifts are nothing without love. That charity is the excellent way that leads most surely to God. . . . I understood that love comprised all vocations, that love was everything, that it embraced all times and places . . . in a word, that it was eternal!" (*Story of a Soul: The Autobiography of St. Thérèse of Lisieux*, trans. John Clarke, 2nd ed. [Washington, DC: ICS Publications, 1976], p. 194).

or state of life, could advance in the spiritual life and grow in holiness. This perspective found a prominent place in chapter 5 of *Lumen gentium*, "The Universal Call to Holiness." In 1985, as the extraordinary synod of bishops celebrated the twentieth anniversary of the Second Vatican Council, they reiterated the theme of the universal call to holiness.[8] Pope John Paul II in his reflection on the Great Jubilee (*Novo millennio ineunte*, 2001) repeated the call of the Council in strong language: "I have no hesitation in saying that all pastoral initiatives must be set in relation to *holiness*. . . . It is necessary, therefore, to rediscover the full practical significance of chapter 5 of the Dogmatic Constitution of the Chuch *Lumen gentium*, dedicated to the 'universal call to holiness.'"[9]

The implications for chapter 4 of *Amoris laetitia* are clear. The title of the chapter "Love in Marriage" contains far more than one might initially think. Love in marriage certainly has to do with the love of the spouses in their marital relationship. In a Christian and sacramental context, however, the growth and development of that particular love embodies the movement toward the perfection, or fulfillment, of the Christian life, whose essence we have come to know is love, because God is love. Since this movement toward perfection and fulfillment belongs to ordinary people in ordinary marriages with ordinary life experiences, we find a verification of the Second Vatican Council's understanding of the universal call to holiness.

Chapter 4, then, ranges well beyond what might be considered a homiletic exhortation. This chapter represents a creative practical spirituality that synthesizes major themes of Christian existence, as they emerged from the renewal of the Second Vatican Council.

---

8. "Because the Church in Christ is mystery, she must be considered a sign and instrument of holiness. For this reason the Council proclaimed the vocation of all the faithful to holiness. The call to holiness is an invitation to an intimate conversion of heart and to participate in the life of God, One and Triune" (4).

9. *Novo millennio ineunte*, 30.

Our Daily Love

Pope Francis uses St. Paul's hymn to love (1 Corinthians 13:4–7) as a point of departure to reflect on the practice of love in ordinary life in the context of marriage and family. He assumes correctly that we learn to love by loving in the particular circumstances and closest relationships of our lives. He also assumes that Paul's description of the aspects of love is both an ideal to be attained and, at the same time, a discipline to be practiced. His approach deserves deeper reflection.

Throughout *Amoris laetitia*, Pope Francis has insisted on the real, and sometimes less than ideal, experiences of people in marriage and family life. This kind of realism is, as we noted earlier, the mark of an authentic spiritual formation process. At the same time, this realistic formation would never move forward unless the ideal were not also included. The Holy Father uses Paul's description of love in two senses. He describes Paul's ideal of love that we strive to attain. At the same time, he presents Paul's description of love as a realistic and lived discipline that moves us ever closer to the ideal.

The following is the text of Paul's teaching that Pope Francis uses:

> Love is patient,
> love is kind;
> love is not jealous or boastful;
> it is not arrogant or rude.
> Love does not insist on its own way,
> it is not irritable or resentful;
> it does not rejoice at wrong,
> but rejoices in the right.
> Love bears all things,
> believes all things,
> hopes all things,
> **endures all things.** (1 Corinthians 13:4-7; cited in n. 90)

Pope Francis' reflections on this hymn to love speak for themselves. We can briefly note some of the essential themes that he attaches to love as an ideal and as a disciplined practice.

Patient . . . love "does not act on impulse and avoids giving offense" (91). *Kind* . . . love "benefits and helps others" (93). *Not jealous* . . . "love values the other person's achievements." *Not boastful* . . . "love is marked by humility" (98). *Not rude* . . . "its actions, words, and gestures are pleasing and not abrasive or rigid" (99). *Generous* . . . love gives "freely and fully" (102). *Not irritable or resentful* . . . love is free from "interior indignation" (103). *Forgives* . . . it is "capable of showing boundless love and forgiving others" (108). *Rejoices with others* . . . love "finds joy in the happiness of others" (110). *Bears all things* . . . love "holds its peace before the limitations of the loved one" (113). *Believes all things* . . . "love trusts, it sets free, it does not try to control" (115). *Hopes all things* . . . love "knows that others can change, mature, and radiate unexpected beauty and untold potential" (116). *Endures all things* . . . love "has a constant readiness to confront any challenge" (118).

Each descriptor of love, in the context of marriage and family life, could be a subject for prayer, reflection, and an examination of conscience. In this way, Paul's words, as Pope Francis presents them, can be a discipline for the practice of growing in love. Each descriptor is also an expression of the ideal of love embodied in the life, death, and Resurrection of Jesus. That ideal is clearly manifest in his self-sacrifice for the ones he loves: "No one has greater love than this, to lay down one's life for one's friends" (John 15:13). We, in turn, move progressively toward the ideal of the complete gift of self, toward that "laying down" of our lives, in the context of marriage and family life. And we do so on a daily basis.

Growing in Conjugal Love

The opening paragraphs of this section (120–122) state that marriage and family life are "growing." This is very significant, because it underscores the journey or process dimension of these human relationships that have a direct connection to our relationship with God. For example, Pope Francis affirms that marriage is the icon of God's love for us, and that it mirrors God's love as well as Christ's love for the Church. These statements seem to propose an ideal that is impossible to attain in an ordinary marriage and an ordinary family. The Holy Father immediately adds that these ideals belong to a process of growth. His words are an invitation to married couples and families to embrace the ideal fully but with the clearheaded recognition that they cannot embrace it and live it fully all at once. "There is no need to lay upon two limited persons the tremendous burden of having to reproduce perfectly the union existing between Christ and his church, for marriage as a sign entails 'a dynamic process . . . one that advances gradually with the progressive integration of the gifts of God'" (122, with a citation from *Familiaris consortio*, 9).

The exhortation develops the ways that the process of growing love unfolds in marriage and family life. For example, the section on lifelong sharing explores marriage as a growing friendship that develops precisely in the measure that it has permanence and continuity. In a word, its growth depends on its definitive character.

The section on joy and beauty applies elements of traditional spirituality—contemplation and the experience of an expanded and joyful heart—to the development of a marriage relationship. This application also explains what it means to grow in married love.

Many young people today, as the pope describes them, do not perceive the joyful, contemplative, and dynamic dimensions of marriage when they think of marriage as a social institution. Instead of something growing and dynamic, the institution of marriage seems staid and numbing, making some young people reluctant to enter into a marriage. Pope Francis addresses this concern in the section on marrying for love. He explains that the dynamic and growth dimensions of married love are not diminished by marriage as a social institution. In fact, the institutionalization of marriage serves to shape, protect, and foster deeper growth in love and commitment.

In a section entitled "a love that reveals itself and increases," Pope Francis offers sensible advice to married couples when he insists that they frequently use the words *please*, *thank you*, and *sorry*. From a formational perspective, his encouragement amounts to much more than helpful advice. He is initiating them to a daily discipline, as any good spiritual guide would do, to foster attention and cultivate the relationship.

The last subsection, "Dialogue," explains that communication carries the relationship forward and enables growth. This is true for the marriage relationship and for one's personal relationship with the Lord when both those relationships come together in living out the Sacrament of Matrimony. The directions for dialogue, which include time, attention, and affection, apply to communications between spouses and prayer directed to the Lord.

Passionate Love

In his teaching on passionate love, Pope Francis draws deeply from the vision of his predecessors Pope John Paul II and Pope Benedict XVI. Both popes insisted on an integral Christian anthropology, a vision of the human person that included all dimensions of what it means to be human. They underscored the importance of emotions and passions, including the erotic dimension of love. All these experiences belong to our humanity.

Amoris laetitia looks to the past and acknowledges limited and sometimes even negative approaches in Church teaching to the emotional and passionate side of life. Pope Francis seeks to remedy that inadequacy as he takes his cue from Pope John Paul II's catechesis on the body and Pope Benedict XVI's *Deus caritas est*, with its affirmation of erotic love. Pope Francis speaks of training while offering a positive formational direction for shaping emotion and instinct. Citing Pope John Paul II, he elaborates on the formative process that this entails:

> To those who fear that the training of the passions and of sexuality detracts from the spontaneity of sexual love, St. John Paul II replied that human persons are "called to full and mature spontaneity in their relationships," a maturity that "is the gradual fruit of a discernment of the impulses of one's own heart." This calls for discipline and self-mastery, since every human person "must learn with perseverance and consistency, the meaning of his or her body."
> (*Amoris laetitia*, 151)

Pope Francis completes this portrait of forming and integrating the emotions with cautions about the shadow side of human sexuality that can be marked by sin: "sexuality risks being poisoned by the mentality of 'use and discard'" (153). Dehumanizing sexuality leads to sexual submission, something that must be rejected. A major part of the formative journey is a process of healing sexuality's wounds, whatever they may be, and integrating a full sense of the human person.

Virginity and celibacy, Pope Francis adds, do not compete with marriage. Rather, these different states of life complement each other. All find their common rooting in a vocation to love, however that will be expressed.

The Transformation of Love

The section "The Transformation of Love" synthesizes the chapter. Two elements make love transformative: a shared and continuous history and a regular reaffirmation of commitment. The power of growth and transformation depend on the cumulative history that a couple shares. Across time, in meeting challenges and joys the couple grows and changes together. That is the power of a shared history. At the same time, their shared history is unsustainable without a continuous reclaiming of their mutual commitment. The regular "repledging" of love enables the spouses to know the essential reliability that they have in each other.

Overall, chapter 4 offers a formational vision, providing a description of grace and, at the same time, of ways of responding to that grace. Reminiscent of the First Letter of John, the chapter seeks to foster love both between the spouses (horizontal love) and with God (vertical love) with the assurance that these two directions are interlocking and, although distinguishable, never separate. A couple's movement toward an ever more perfect union with each other brings them to an ever more perfect union with God. Their union with God substantially moves their union with each other ever closer.

☀ Questions for Reflection

1. How does *Amoris laetitia* reorient the Church to an understanding of what love can be.

2. How necessary is the reclaiming of love for our world and culture?

3. How can married couples and families find the love that they have for each other reflected in the history and traditions of the Church?

6

Accompanying, Discerning, and Integrating Weakness

Each marriage is a kind of "salvation history," which from fragile beginnings—thanks to God's gift and a creative and generous response on our part—grows over time into something precious and enduring.

—*Amoris laetitia, 221*

Chapter 8 of *Amoris laetitia* touches on the sensitive issues of divorce, civil remarriage, and admission to the Eucharist. One could read this chapter searching for a change in doctrine or moral teaching or sacramental discipline to accommodate people who find themselves in difficult situations. In that search, the larger context of *Amoris laetitia* is lost. Although the exhortation presupposes doctrinal, moral, and disciplinary dimensions of marriage, it does not break new ground in these areas. Its fundamental proposal is to offer the People of God a path of formation in the ordinary life that most people lead—in their marriages and with their families.

The chapter title indicates the three formational activities of accompaniment, discernment, and integration. As they are developed in the chapter, these activities involve the formation and exercise of conscience. Conscience certainly addresses situations of weakness or what is "irregular." However, conscience has a much larger role in marriage and family life. On a daily basis, decisions are made and directions taken in families and marriages that have a significant impact. How do we do this in the right way, that is, the way that best expresses our following of Jesus Christ as his disciples? Conscience plays its decisive role in these decisions and directions, helping us to resolve thorny moral issues and enabling us to embrace the positive direction of our lives that leads us to love God and each other.

A good starting point for reflecting on conscience can be found in two paragraphs of the *Catechism of the Catholic Church*. Paragraph 1776 draws from *Gaudium et spes*, 16. It reads:

> Deep within his conscience man discovers a law which he has not laid upon himself but which he must obey. Its voice, ever calling him to love and to do what is good and to avoid evil, sounds in his heart at the right moment. . . . For man has in his heart a law inscribed by God. . . . His conscience is man's most secret core and his sanctuary. There he is alone with God whose voice echoes in his depths.

Paragraph 1777 describes how conscience functions.

> Moral conscience, present at the heart of the person, enjoins him at the appropriate moment to do good and to avoid evil. It also judges particular choices, approving those that are good and denouncing those that are evil. It bears witness to the authority of truth in reference to the supreme Good to which the human person is drawn, and it welcomes the commandments. When he listens to his conscience, the prudent man can hear God speaking.

Frequently, people do not have a good grasp of conscience. Some see it as a cold, almost bureaucratic, technical application of law. It is enough, they might say, to know what is right and then just do it. For others, conscience is something very different. It is about a subjective judgment. What matters, in their estimation, is how they feel about something. Conscience, then, becomes a matter of accommodation. For example, I could feel comfortable knowing that what I am doing may not be the right thing, but, "in conscience," I can live with it. This kind of conscience is never fully formed, and it has no deep rooting. It easily becomes a kind of escape hatch.[1]

---

1. James F. Keenan, "Redeeming Conscience," in *Theological Studies* 76/1 (March 2015), p. 135.

Pastorally, it is unwise to say to someone, "Just follow your conscience." What conscience, indeed, are they going to follow? This dilemma underscores the need to help with the formation of conscience. Pope Francis speaking to the whole Church in *Amoris laetitia* says, "We have been called to form consciences, not to replace them" (37).

Seven Steps in the Formation of Conscience

1. Beginning with distress. Beginning with distress means that a person (or a community, for that matter) experiences a genuine moral dilemma, struggle, or ambiguity. Even if a question of sin is not in play, but rataher the more general question of doing God's will in a given situation, there may be some distress or tension. Anyone who is clear and convinced about the rightness or wrongness of a given decision or action will not be exercising conscience. If, for example, he or she is convinced that something is wrong but wants to "check with my conscience," it is likely that this person is looking for an escape hatch.

Genuine distress is also absent when an individual rationalizes something that they clearly understand as wrong but then transform it into a good to be embraced. Pope Francis addresses this when he says:

> Naturally, if someone flaunts an objective sin as if it were part
> of the Christian ideal or wants to impose something other than
> what the church teaches, he or she can in no way presume to
> teach or preach to others; this is a case of something that sepa-
> rates from the community (cf. Mt. 18:17). Such a person needs to
> listen once more to the gospel message and its call to conversion.
> (*Amoris laetitia*, 297)

These examples illustrate a false sense of distress. A true sense of distress, dilemma, struggle, or ambiguity emerges in our experience differently. I may, for example, experience a tension between a clearly enunciated value that I know and accept as correct and the way that my life does not fit into that ideal for whatever reason. That genuine sense of distress leads into the second step.

2. The driving question. We know that the exercise of true conscience is not equivalent to the technical application of a rule to a given situation nor is it equivalent to subjective judgment based on inclinations in the moment. The driving question in the exercise of conscience cannot be reduced to: "What is the law that is to be applied?" Nor can it be: "How do I feel about it?"

If conscience, as *Gaudium et spes* and the *Catechism* both state, means being "alone with God whose voice echoes in (the person's) depths" (CCC, 1776), the driving question takes a particular shape. It must be: "Where is God calling me? Or, where is God drawing me?"

From my encounter with the living God in the given circumstances and possibilities of my life, what is God asking of me? This is the question that a conscience struggling to identify the right thing to do must ask. That kind of question prompts a process of honest, real, open, and courageous searching. It assumes that we can find ourselves in circumstances and situations that do not yield immediate clarity. Often this lack of immediate clarity derives from the more detailed and more specific circumstances of our lives that are less susceptible to resolution by general rules and standards. Pope Francis cites Thomas Aquinas to this effect in paragraph 304 of *Amoris laetitia*:

> Although there is necessity in the general principles, the more we
> descend to matters of detail, the more frequently we encounter
> defects. . . . In matters of action, truth or practical rectitude is
> not the same for all, as to matters of detail, but only as to the gen-
> eral principles; and where there is the same rectitude in matters
> of detail, it is not equally known to all. . . . The principle will
> be found to fail, according as we descend further into detail.
> (*Summa theologiae I-II*, q. 94, a. 4)

3. Conscience in constant formation in the Church. As we consider the personal and highly specific dimensions of conscience, some questions may naturally arise. For example, what saves us from being merely subjective in our judgments? What prevents us from fooling ourselves and following a path of least resistance?

To respond to these valid questions, we need to return to the absolutely personal character of conscience. Recall the words of the *Catechism*: "For man has in his heart a law inscribed by God. . . . His conscience is man's most secret core and his sanctuary" (1776). Conscience is absolutely personal and belongs to each of us as a gift of God. At the same time, it does not exist in a merely private domain detached and disengaged from everything and everyone. When the *Catechism* speaks of the formation of conscience, it introduces us to a larger-than-personal world:

> In the formation of conscience the Word of God is the light for our path; we must assimilate it in faith and prayer and put it into practice. We must also examine our conscience before the Lord's Cross. We are assisted by the gifts of the Holy Spirit, aided by the witness or advice of others and guided by the authoritative teaching of the Church. (*Catechism of the Catholic Church*, 1785)

The personal and individual dimension of conscience, discernment, and moral decision-making rightly occupies a central position in our understanding. This personal dimension, however, fits into the larger context of Christian existence. Especially in our culture that prizes the individual and individual choice, we need to recall the corporate and communitarian shape of our journey to God. *Lumen gentium* expresses this reality clearly: "At all times and in every race, anyone who fears God and does what is right has been acceptable to him. . . . He has, however, willed to make men [and women] holy and save them, not as individuals without any bond or link between them, but rather to make them into a people who might acknowledge him and serve him in holiness" (9).

Conscience continuously develops in relationship to the larger community of faith, the Church. What does this mean in the practical order of things? In a number of significant ways, the Church contributes to the formation of conscience and our capacity to discern what is right and wrong and what is to be decided and done. The Church proclaims and teaches norms and values that belong to the core of Christian existence. For example, as the Church proposes justice, compassion, fidelity, mercy, and reconciliation as central directions for all disciples of

Jesus, the consciences of individual believers recognize the ideals and standards to which they are called.

The formation of conscience is also tied to the essential dimensions of the Church's ministry: Word, sacrament, and service to the world. When individual believers have contact with this core of the Church's ministry, they have a direct and formative experience that shapes their general awareness and their consciences. To hear the Word is to receive God's communication and not only in a generic sense but as applicable to our particular circumstances. To share in the sacramental life of the Church means encountering and joining Christ in the saving mysteries of his death and Resurrection. To know the service of the Church to the world, that Church which is "in the manner of a sacrament of the unity of all humanity in God,"[2] shapes in us a new and urgent sense of responsibility for our action in the world. In this way, contact with the core of the Church's ministry—Word, sacrament, service—forms and shapes our consciences.

The community of faith, the Church, is a place of encounter. Believers meet each other, are in dialogue with one another, and sometimes work together. When we meet each other at the deeper levels of our lives, for example, in the context of profound suffering, loss, or a struggle to find a life direction, we exercise a formative effect on each other. Our consciences are formed in and through these living encounters that represent shared accompaniment and discernment, even if we do not have the vocabulary to name them as such.

The Church is also far more than the sum of people who are now living. The Church is a historical people of faith and a living Communion of Saints. The witness of others who have gone before us marked with the sign of faith has inestimable value for our formation and for our life directions. The great charity and generosity, lived out both within their homes and in their cities, of Sts. Elizabeth of Hungary and Frances of Rome establish a formative witness to shape our consciences today.

---

2. *Lumen gentium*, 1.

The same is true for Maximilian Kolbe, who offered his life so another could live.

This section began with the perplexing questions: How can conscience, which is indeed so personal and so individual, be saved from being merely subjective? What can prevent us from self-deception? What helps us to embrace true and objective values? The answer to these questions rests in the ongoing formation of conscience in the Church. The Church provides reliable teaching about norms and values, a direct experience of Word, sacrament, and service, a place of encounter with other believers, and the historical witness of great men and women of faith.

4. Steps of a decision-making process. Whether we need to determine if something is right or wrong or if we need to determine what might be the most faithful direction for our discipleship, conscience can guide us. It does so in a process. The four steps that follow identify basic elements of that process.

a. Although feelings accompany any significant decision-making process, they are transitory and, therefore, ought not to be the main driver of a decision. If we expect some durability for what we decide, we need to turn to knowledge. With all rational people of good will, we know and share common values and standards—for example, not wanting to inflict harm on others. Additionally as believers, we have distinct knowledge of values embedded in our existence as disciples of Jesus Christ, the place of mercy in a wounded world, and our responsibility to share it.

The way that we hold knowledge needs to be distinguished. Our knowledge of values and standards is general and theoretical. We can know "in theory" what is right and what is to be done. There is, however, another and more immediately relevant kind of knowledge for decision-making. In our moral tradition, that knowledge is called "estimative" or "evaluative." This knowledge bridges theoretical understanding with the personal realm of my life and existence. Not only do I know that something is true in general, but with estimative knowledge, I also perceive it as true for me in my context.

A New Vision of Family Life

b. A second moment is reckoning with our freedom. We must be free to make decisions and take directions; otherwise, those decisions and directions do not belong to us. It is essential, however, to identify with precision the kind of freedom we have. Some people function as if they were entirely free to decide or to move as they wish without qualification. These people live with an illusion. Many factors, from genetics to cultural conditioning, do not allow us to claim absolute freedom. On the other side of the question of freedom, many assert that there is no freedom at all and that we are entirely determined in our decisions and actions. These people also live under an illusion that not only diminishes personal responsibility but removes it entirely. Between the two assertions of absolute freedom and no freedom at all is a realistic middle ground. We are free, but we enjoy a conditioned freedom. At the core of our lives, we have a certain freedom to direct ourselves in a path of self-giving or, alternately, a path of closing ourselves off from others.

In making decisions and taking important directions in our lives, we need to reckon with the freedom that we possess. We also need to take into account what impinges on and limits that freedom.

c. The third step is to make a decision or to take a direction. With knowledge and freedom, we decide. In that decision, we take responsibility and claim ownership for it. As we accept responsibility, we accept the consequences or results of the decision.

d. The final step in this process is to surrender ourselves into the hands of our merciful God. When our decision involves a weighty matter of morality or life direction, we are understandably concerned with whether we have made the right decision. Even more, we are concerned that with the decision, we stand right before God. Because our knowledge and our freedom are imperfect, we can never be entirely certain that we have made the best, or even the correct, decision. Self-doubt can plague us and even breed agony in a scrupulous person. For all of us, there will be at least some concern and perhaps some anxiety. At this point, when we have done the best that we can with what we have, we are summoned to an act of trust and surrender into the hands of God, who is mercy.

For some people, this last step of the process is the most difficult and may even be impossible. Their thirst for certitude is such that they cannot let go of the decision and surrender it into God's merciful hands. Their need for clarity and certitude may drive them to understand conscience as a technical application of a rule to a given situation. That technical approach, in its own mistaken way, offers a path of certitude that avoids risk.

These four steps of the process give us a broad outline of how we come to make important decisions or take directions with the help of conscience. A consideration of pastoral and personal discernment fills out the process of exercising conscience.

5. Pastoral discernment. Discernment has a long history in Christian spirituality and moral formation. In the New Testament, it appears in Paul's writings and in the First Letter of John. The earliest monastics, the fathers and mothers of the desert, practiced it and wrote about it, as did St. Ignatius of Loyola in the *Spiritual Exercises*. How, then, does the biblical and spiritual tradition describe discernment?

In spiritual literature, the full phrase is "discernment of spirits." Discernment assumes that spirits, or movements, are at work in our lives. Some of these spirits and movements tend to move us away from God, and others bring us closer to God. It is important to sort out these movements so that we can go more freely and more generously in directions and promptings from God. The operations of conscience draw on the process of discernment to identify right directions. Finally, discernment as a gift of the Holy Spirit attunes us to what is good, sometimes to what is better, and always to what is of God.

A fuller understanding of discernment requires that it be distinguished from diagnosis. Making a diagnosis involves the application of our intellects and a process of reasoning. In other words, we figure things out and then apply a remedy or solution to a given question or problematic situation. The diagnostic model has a formulaic quality.

Discernment operates much differently. Rather than thinking things out, discernment begins with the conviction that God is already moving in a situation or in our lives. If we wait and watch properly and are attuned to the signs of God's presence, God's truth will emerge as something to be discovered. The biblical-spiritual tradition has identified various signs of God's presence or movement. One of the simplest and most direct can be found in the words of Jesus: "By their fruits, you shall know them" (Matthew 7:16; see Luke 6:44).

Discernment figures prominently in *Amoris laetitia*. It is linked, for example, to sorting out the possibilities latent in complex marriage and family situations. Given the possibilities and the limitations of a given situation, discernment asks, What is the best possible response that God would want from these people?

The exhortation encourages pastoral discernment. Often this means that a priest accompanies a family on its journey. Or it could mean that a couple married for many years make themselves available to younger couples as they seek to navigate the challenging early years of marriage and family life. Pastoral discernment, whatever form it takes, accompanies people. Sometimes teaching and wisdom are offered from experience and from the tradition. At all times in pastoral discernment, those being accompanied are encouraged to make their own discernment. Those accompanying others during pastoral discernment never dictate a direction and certainly never replace another person's judgment.

For pastoral discernment to prompt the discernment process in others, questions may be taken up that foster reflection, prayer, and watchfulness. Among these questions might be: Given your situation and capacities, what do you sense God is asking of you in this moment? How can you—in your admittedly limited circumstances—be faithful? How do you move, as St. Thomas speaks of it, from the general to the more and more particular? How will you move to ever greater fidelity and ever closer to the ideal? What are the positive elements of a situation that overall does not match the ideal? How can you build on these and move forward, never losing sight of the ideal?

These questions certainly do not exhaust all the possibilities of help that can be rendered through pastoral discernment, but they indicate a path of accompaniment. One person or a group serves others on their journey. The ones who offer pastoral discernment and accompaniment remain as a steadfast and faithful presence to others. Their words may be questions, as we see here, or a challenge or encouragement to continue the journey.

6. Personal discernment. Pastoral discernment is the help that one or several believers give to others who are on the journey of faith. In the end, those believers on the journey must claim ownership for their process, decisions, and directions. Personal discernment belongs to them. They may benefit from pastoral discernment and accompaniment, but at a certain moment they must assume responsibility.

Note that personal discernment is not private. The larger community of faith both facilitates and supports it. There is no opposition between the personal and communal, especially in matters of faith.

7. The places where the Church offers accompaniment and discernment. The Church offers the help of accompaniment and discernment in two privileged places: the non-sacramental internal forum and the sacramental forum of the Sacrament of Penance. Each forum has its particular features.

The internal nonsacramental forum is a place of privileged encounter between two believers. This encounter may take the form of spiritual direction or pastoral counseling or even, more simply, a confidential dialogue of spiritual support. The believer who is grappling with a decision or direction seeks the help of another believer. The ensuing dialogue considers the dimensions of a challenging situation that call for decision and action. The entire exchange takes place in a mutually agreed upon confidentiality that precludes disclosure to anyone outside of the relationship. In an atmosphere of frank trust, then, these two believers together try to listen to where God may be leading the person who has come for help. The atmosphere of confidentiality coupled with a mutually shared trust in the action of God when "two or three come together" in the name of Jesus (Matthew 18:20) allow for free exploration and expression. Depending on the circumstances, this may not be a one-time occasion. The required discernment and accompaniment more often will mean a series of meetings over time. If there are no preset time or session limits, both believers will sense the freedom to give the situation under consideration its due attention. Of course, this does not mean endless sessions and a permanent lack of resolution. It is precisely the task of accompaniment and discernment—at the right time—to call the question and invite a decision.

The other place for accompaniment and discernment is the sacramental forum of the Sacrament of Penance. In this instance, a penitent approaches a priest to celebrate the sacrament. In the course of their dialogue, the penitent presents the situation that prompts some exploration and discernment. Of course, because of the seal of confession, this sacramental conversation has a completely confidential character. That enables a free exchange. There are, however, some significant limitations in the sacramental forum. There are time constraints, especially if other penitents are waiting to approach the sacrament, and usually this is a one-time conversation. Whatever needs to be considered must be considered in this single encounter. At the same time, the sacramental forum can be an avenue of discernment and accompaniment, and it is recognized as such by the Church. Because this encounter takes place in the context of the Sacrament of Penance, the key for the confessor and the penitent is a determination of the penitent's repentance that seeks reintegration in the life of the Church, the Body of Christ. If the penitent does not seem to be genuinely repentant, then it may be necessary to have the penitent return another time after a period of further prayer and reflection. In general, because of the inherent limitations of the sacramental forum, a confessor is well advised to urge his penitent to take his or her concerns, especially if they are complicated and have a long history, to the nonsacramental forum. There, the person seeking assistance can find more time and greater attention.

Care for the Divorced and Remarried

The painful marital situations that fall under the category of "irregular" do not fully embody the ideal. *Amoris laetitia* makes an important contribution in addressing these situations. Pope Francis clearly holds up the ideal of marriage and family life in the context of exclusivity, permanence, fidelity, and generativity. At the same time, he urgently and insistently tells the Church and her ministers that they must never abandon those who do not fully live out the ideal. Just as there is always room for God's grace and mercy to work in the lives of people, so there is always room for the Church's ministry to reach out and serve people who find themselves in these irregular situations. But how exactly can the Church serve people in these difficult and often delicate situations? After considering several presuppositions of caring for people in irregular situations, we will note a number of steps that the Church can take in a specific process of discernment and accompaniment.

A first presupposition: there are no precise formulas. The human condition is always complex and no more so than in marriage and family life. Each relationship carries its own complexity. Each marriage and family must be viewed on its own terms. Citing both the synod report and Pope Benedict XVI, Pope Francis says, "There is a need 'to avoid judgments that do not take into account the complexity of various situations' and 'to be attentive, by necessity, to how people experience distress because of their condition'" (296).

Sometimes, in a desire for clarity and precision, those serving couples may move in a rigorist fashion. This involves clear and strict applications of laws and regulations. On the other side, some of those serving couples follow a laxist path. With such a path, there is no attention and little care for those values of permanence, fidelity, and generativity that Jesus proclaimed concerning marriage. The laxist way seeks easy resolution and accommodation. Unfortunately, neither the rigorist nor the laxist approach takes into honest account the demands of the Gospel and the demands of complicated human situations.

Since there are no precise formulas, and since neither rigorist nor laxist approaches are adequate, what is required for ministers to married couples in difficult situations and for the couples themselves? Pope Francis cites the final report of the synod, saying, "For this discernment to happen, the following conditions must necessarily be present: humility, discretion, and love for the church and her teaching, in a sincere search for God's will and a desire to make a more perfect response to it" (300).

Finally, concerning the lack of precise formulas that could be applied to a given situation, Pope Francis, in paragraph 304, turns to St. Thomas Aquinas:

> Although there is necessity in the general principles, the more we descend to matters of detail, the more frequently we encounter defects. . . . In matters of action, truth or practical rectitude is not the same for all, as to matters of detail, but only as to the general principles and where there is the same rectitude in matters of detail, it is not equally known to all. . . . The principle will be found to fail, according as we descend further into detail.

A second presupposition: the law of gradualism. Pope Francis, in *Amoris laetitia*, and Pope John Paull II, in *Familiaris consortio*, speak of the law of gradualism. They are insistent that there is a process, often a gradual process, by which we move forward in embracing and integrating moral and spiritual truth. Describing gradualism, Pope Francis writes:

> St. John Paul II proposed the so-called "law of gradualness" in the knowledge that the human being "knows, loves, and accomplishes moral good by different stages of growth." This is not a "gradualness of law" but rather a gradualness in the prudential exercise of free acts on the part of subjects who are not in a position to understand, appreciate, or fully carry out the objective demands of the law. . . . For the law is itself a gift of God that points out the way, a gift for everyone without exception; it can be followed with the help of grace, even though each human being "advances gradually with the progressive integration of the gifts of God and the demands of God's definitive and absolute love in his or her entire personal and social life." (*Amoris laetitia*, 295)

The dynamic context for Christian formation is verified in the law of gradualism. All of us are pilgrims, on a journey going home to God. Along the way, we navigate the best we can until we arrive. This side of death, however, we will continue to be on the way. That sense of movement is contained in the law of gradualism. All of this would seem to be unarguable, a pattern of growth echoed in other aspects of human development. However, a strain of Christian spirituality stands in sharp contrast to the law of gradualism. As noted earlier, the whole horizon for the moral and spiritual life is set by the poles of "state of sin" and "state of grace." In this mindset, one is called to repent and move out of the state of sin that means alienation from God and eternal damnation. At the same time, one is called to embrace and cultivate the state of grace, the indwelling of the Triune God through sanctifying grace as well as the possibility of being admitted to eternal bliss and the beatific vision. Above all, the great desire and quest for Christians is simply this: to be found in the state of grace at the moment of death. Although some of this was considered earlier, it deserves to be revisited because of its importance.

First, "state of sin" and "state of grace" portray a reality. There is a state of sin, because we have the capacity to push away from God and to be frozen in our alienation. There is a state of grace, because we can—even in this life—share in the very life of God, Father, Son, and Holy Spirit. When these two states become the exclusive horizon for the Christian life, then they present something real but also incomplete. The words "state of" imply a reality that is static. Some approaches to spirituality in our recent past and perhaps among some people today are tinged with Jansenism. When that is the case, the spiritual life is reduced to snapping out of the state of sin and snapping into the state of grace and vice versa. This automaton-like approach to grace belies its power and its subtlety. One may be in a state of sin and—contrary to the Jansenist position—be moved, little by little, by actual grace to repentance and a conversion of heart. Of course, movement can be in the opposite direction as well. One may be in the state of grace, but little by little, the corrosive work of sin can draw the person away from God until there is full-blown alienation.

The law of gradualism suggests that there is much, much more to the Christian story than jumping in and out of the state of sin or the state of grace. There is a wider, longer, sometimes more circuitous route than we might have imagined. It is a journey, after all, and one that bears all the struggles and successes of any significant journey.

A third presupposition: the ever-present and ever-operative mercy of God. The formational context for *Amoris laetitia* is quite simply the mercy of God. Pope Francis has steadily reiterated God's abundant mercy as the key to the Christian life. In this sense, mercy is not just one dimension among others of the Christian journey. Mercy informs every step of the journey. In no place is this truer than in marriage and family life. Mercy thaws frozen relationships with God and with others. Mercy unties the knots of tangled relationships. In effect, the mercy of God mediated by the Church is the instrument of last resort that provides a lifeline to those in desperate situations. Of course, that mercy must be accepted as grace and gift in a spirit of true repentance. With that acceptance comes the responsibility to live the gift.

A sample passage in *Amoris laetitia* captures this essential mercy in the context of difficult situations:

> It is a matter of reaching out to everyone, of needing to help each person find his or her proper way of participating in the ecclesial community and thus to experience being touched by an "unmerited, unconditional, and gratuitous" mercy. No one can be condemned forever, because that is not the logic of the gospel! Here I am not speaking only of the divorced and remarried but of everyone in whatever situation they find themselves. (*Amoris laetitia*, 297)

The Steps of Integration

The Church's ministry helps people in difficult or irregular situations to "find his or her proper way of participating in the ecclesial community and thus to experience being touched by . . . mercy" (297). Notice that this discernment is about integration into the life of the believing community. "Integration" is a wider category than readmitting those who are divorced and civilly remarried to the sacraments. "Integration" is the third term of the triad of the title of chapter 8: "Accompanying, Discerning, and Integrating Weakness." Whatever ministry of accompaniment and discernment that the Church offers, it is always oriented toward the integration of believers in one way or another into the life of the Church. That integration, in certain circumstances, may mean readmission to the sacraments. It also may mean other forms of participation in the life of the Church that can—one would hope—eventually lead to full sacramental integration. Unfortunately, these subtleties and nuances are often lost in a rush to resolve difficult situations.

How exactly is this integration achieved? What are the elements of pastoral and personal accompaniment and discernment that foster that achievement? We can respond to these important questions by identifying a series of steps to be taken. These steps are drawn from *Amoris laetitia* as well as from the practical pastoral wisdom of the Church, for example, as has developed in the *praxis confessorum*, the confessional practice of those who minister the Sacrament of Penance.

Step 1: Recognition of "irregularity." The word "irregularity" covers a wide swath of situations from those that include a lack of recognition by the Church because of a formality to the more serious "objective state of sin," that is, the assessment based on external evidence that persons do not conform to God's plan. This objective state of sin, as we shall later see, may or may not correspond to subjective guilt because of a variety of circumstances.

The recognition of irregularity by those who find themselves in such a situation is fundamental for any process that eventually seeks integration into the life of the Church. At various times, Pope Francis speaks of people feeling "distress." In other words, people recognize that something is not correct about their situation or arrangement. They understand that their situation does not match the ideals of the Gospel and the teaching and practice of the Church. This distress breeds a grieving and, sometimes, a sense of dilemma, isolation, or even alienation.

Distress and its byproducts seem to be negative. In one sense, they are. At the same time in a more positive direction, the distress generated by the felt variance from the ideal can prompt people to take a second look at their lives. This contrasts with the attitude of indifference that declares that whatever the situation is, it does not matter. It also stands in contrast to those who seek to justify their situation, as if there were a positive good and then flaunt "an objective sin as if it were part of the Christian ideal," as Pope Francis notes in paragraph 297.

The recognition of irregularity and the concomitant feeling of distress are fundamental experiences on the journey to integration. Without these, there is no motivation and no reason to move forward.

Step 2: Willingness and ability to use ordinary means. For couples who are divorced and remarried, the ordinary path of recourse to regularize their union is through a declaration of nullity. This is pursued through a canonical process. If a declaration of nullity for their previous union(s) is granted, the couple's union is celebrated in the Church.[3]

If the couple feels that they cannot be bothered to pursue a canonical process or they seek some form of personal exception through an internal forum solution, then the Church can legitimately question their sincerity. A basic willingness to follow an ordinary process is fundamental in pursuing the process of integration.

The couple may be willing to follow the process but unable to do so for various reasons. For example, they may live in a place that, effectively speaking, does not have a functioning ecclesiastical tribunal. The tribunal may be so understaffed or inefficient that cases languish for years. It may also happen that a petitioner feels unable to pay for the

---

3. There is an ordinary process for those seeking a declaration of nullity in the *Code of Canon Law*. Additionally, in light of the two synods on the family, Pope Francis has issued two motu proprios (*Mitis Iudex Dominus Iesus* and *Mitis et misericors Iesus*) that, in certain circumstances, allow for a streamlined process judged by the diocesan bishop. See his audience with the participants in the course promoted by the Tribunal of the Roman Rota (November 25, 2017). Ample formal resources and opportunities should be available for petitioners.

cost of the tribunal process, even though the law provides for gratuitous coverage of legal expenses in cases of necessity. Finally, for a variety of reasons, it may be impossible to establish grounds for the declaration of nullity in an ecclesiastical tribunal, although in fact and in conscience, the petitioner is completely convinced of the invalidity of the first bond of marriage. Other circumstances also may foreclose the possibility of a canonical process, for example, a hostile government that impedes such ecclesiastical processes.

The second step involves the determination of the willingness of a couple to pursue the ordinary means that the Church offers for reintegration into the community of faith. Even for couples who are willing, it may not always be possible to follow these ordinary means. In that case, a discernment must be made to identify reasons why the ordinary procedure cannot be followed. With this in order, the couple can move to the next step.

Step 3: A sincere and honest examination of conscience. A very important step on the way to integration is a sincere and honest examination of conscience. This is an appraisal of one's history and current situation. Pope Francis cites the final synod report in describing the kinds of questions that people might bring to such an act of self-reflection:

> The divorced and remarried should ask themselves: How did they act toward their children when the conjugal union entered into crisis; whether or not they made attempts at reconciliation; what has become of the abandoned party; what consequences the new relationship has on the rest of the family and the community of the faithful; and what example is being set for young people who are preparing for marriage. Sincere reflection can strengthen trust in the mercy of God, which is not denied anyone. (*Amoris laetitia*, 300)

These questions assume that divorce and remarriage have an impact that ranges beyond the married partners. Children, extended family, and the community of faith all need to be considered. Even more significantly, these questions assume that calling, in trust, on the mercy of God means first knowing one's need for forgiveness. It is not possible to open a new chapter of integration or reintegration into the community of faith without an honest sense of one's history, of all that has led to and culminated in this moment. This kind of retrieval also contributes to an ability to repair and to heal whatever has been damaged. Finally, it illuminates possibilities for a future that avoids the mistakes, hurts, and sins of the past.

Some people are reluctant to dredge up the unpleasant past, and for that reason do not want to pursue a canonical process. They feel that they have moved on in their life and, therefore, do not want to revisit old, painful stories. In fact, the life and relationship appraisal signaled by this third step can be both liberating for the future and healing in the present moment. It does, however, take courage to embark on this step. Here again, the Church's ministry serves an indispensable role through an accompaniment and discernment to support and encourage this necessary step.

Step 4: A review of the current situation. The process of accompanied discernment looks not only to the past but also to the current moment and to the future. In a particular way, this means viewing the current situation in all its particularity and avoiding at all costs a premature categorization of the situation and the people involved. Discernment upholds the principles and values of the Gospel and Church teaching but recognizes that these realities can only come alive in the particular details and shape of peoples' lives.

Pope Francis describes this review of one's current situation with an eye to discerning a direction for the future.

> The divorced who have entered a new union, for example, can find themselves in a variety of situations that should not be pigeonholed or fit into overly rigid classifications leaving no room for personal and pastoral discernment. One thing is a second union consolidated over time, with new children, proven fidelity, generous self-giving, Christian commitment, a consciousness of its irregularity and of the great difficulty of going back without feeling in conscience that one would fall into new sins. (*Amoris laetitia*, 298)

This review becomes, in effect, a gauge of the work of grace or its absence in a given relationship and set of circumstances. The spiritual truth of the relationship sets the context for making important decisions.

Step 5: A fundamental decision to stay or to separate. In the past, persons who were married in the Church and who presumably established a sacramental union and then divorced and remarried another person civilly seemed to have limited choices if they wished to be fully integrated into the life of the Church. In fact, the single option available to them was to separate from their current partner. Pope John Paul II, in his apostolic exhortation *Familiaris consortio*, broke new ground and expanded the choices available to divorced and remarried people. Pope Francis cites him in *Amoris laetitia* to this effect: "The church acknowledges situations 'where for serious reasons, such as the children's upbringing, a man and a woman cannot satisfy the obligation to separate'" (298). If they do not separate but live together according to *Familiaris consortio*, then they are to live as brother and sister, that is, they are to abstain from sexual relations with each other.

Clearly, the ideal in *Familiaris consortio* is separation, but particular circumstances allow the couple to remain together, share a life together, and raise children together. In effect, they share the basic description of marriage as a *consortium vitae*, a life partnership,[4] in every aspect except that of sexual relations. That provision of abstaining from sexual relations is what allows them to participate fully, that is, sacramentally, in the life of the Church. In this provision, it seems that Pope John Paul II recognized that the complexity of certain situations does not allow for a full embrace of the ideal as the tradition had proposed it and that other moral claims (for example, responsibility toward the children of the union) need to shape basic life decisions.

---

4. This description of marriage as *consortium vitae* is based on what we read in *Gaudium et spes*, 48, and what we find explicitly in canon 1055, par. 1, and in the *Catechism of the Catholic Church*, 1601.

At this point, we come to a critical point in *Amoris laetitia* in the text of the exhortation at paragraph 305 and in footnote 351. The relevant text reads: "Because of forms of conditioning and mitigating factors, it is possible that in an objective situation of sin—which may not be subjectively culpable, or fully such—a person can be living in God's grace, can love and can also grow in the life of grace and charity, while receiving the Church's help to this end." The footnote to that passage reads: "In certain cases, this can include the help of the sacraments. . . . I would also point out that the Eucharist 'is not a prize for the perfect, but a powerful medicine and nourishment for the weak'" (footnote 351). In effect, Pope Francis seems to suggest that a divorced and remarried couple who, for good reasons, continue to live together (and do so for reasons identified by Pope John Paul II) may also include sexual relations and still be able to be admitted to the Eucharist in a way not envisioned by Pope John Paul II. Is there a doctrinal or moral change in these words of *Amoris laetitia*, or is there a development from *Familiaris consortio* to *Amoris laetitia*?

First, it is essential to note that *Amoris laetitia* does not change the doctrinal or moral teaching of the Church's tradition in any way. Pope Francis, for example, speaks of "an objective situation of sin," that is, two people still bound by previous and presumably valid marriage bonds now living together as man and wife. He does not identify this as a neutral situation and, even less, as a good one. It carries an objective disorder, that is, sin. Sin, however, does not have a life of its own. Sin is always embodied in the life of a person. Although there may be something objectively wrong, subjective culpability (think full knowledge and free consent) may not correspondingly be present. That opens a path, in this case, for sacramental participation.

Because this development in *Amoris laetitia* is often poorly understood, and because some writers have set Pope Francis in opposition to Pope John Paul II, these questions need to be considered in greater detail. The following paragraphs cite the study of Father Basilio Petrà, who, in my estimation, has convincingly demonstrated the continuity of *Amoris laetitia* with the doctrinal tradition and with the Church's sacramental practice. He writes:

> There is a fundamental principle that is implicitly assumed in the text of *Familiaris consortio* that leads to the exclusion of those who are divorced and remarried from the Eucharist. This principle *substantially* underwrites the exclusion which is expressed in general terms. The principle is this: you can *never* admit to the Eucharist anyone who is living an objective contradiction to what is objectively signified in the Eucharist.

> Still, you cannot find the principle articulated *in such an absolute form* in the tradition. Actually, one can decisively affirm that the tradition and the moral practice of the church do not recognize this kind of absolutizing in the practical moral realm.

> Part of the moral tradition, in fact, is the whole patrimony of the *praxis confessarii* [confessional practice]. And this part of the tradition across time has offered broader perspectives and different kinds of outcomes than might be suggested by the way the principle is enunciated in *Familiaris consortio*. For example, this *praxis* knows that to offer absolution, you cannot ask more of the penitent than the penitent is capable of giving. There are circumstances in which you cannot ask a penitent—for purposes of absolution or admission to Holy Communion—to separate himself/herself from a situation of significant moral danger, if, for example, this would involve provoking serious damage to himself/herself, or to his or her loved ones, or to persons for whom the penitent has serious responsibilities. In this context, moral theology speaks of "necessary proximate occasions of sin." And so, the tradition is acquainted with circumstances that indicate that *you ought not to try to change* a person's objectively wrong opinions or assessments on the way to absolution and admission to the Eucharist. In these instances, the person does not know or cannot understand the truth of certain moral positions that the church takes. In these circumstances, penitents are in a state of "invincible ignorance" or in the condition of a "subjectively defensible conscience" (keeping in mind what we considered about grave sin). When people find themselves in such circumstances, the confessor makes an assessment, keeping in mind the good of the penitent, and the confessor

A New Vision of Family Life

can absolve the penitent and admit him/her to the Eucharist. This is possible, even if the confessor knows that the penitent's lived situation (that is, the penitent's behavior) is, as far as the church is concerned, an objective disorder. The tradition is well aware of the situation of a *perplexed conscience*. That is the case of a person who recognizes in his/her conscience that however they act or decide, they will do evil. At the same time, they cannot refrain from acting. In this case, Catholic moral theology has always affirmed that the person is called to choose the lesser evil. And furthermore, in choosing this lesser evil, the person is not culpable. . . .

These positions of confessional *praxis*, which are solidly present in Catholic moral history, *do not negate the principle used by Familiaris consortio but neither do they absolutize it*. Rather, these positions continually interpret that principle and subject it to the "economy" of salvation—as Eastern theologians might say—in relationship to real concrete people and their Christian journey.

Again, these positions of confessional praxis attest that the tradition considered in its widest range has admitted and does admit persons to Eucharistic communion even in some cases in which there is a lack of consistency between their objective situation and the objective meaning of the Eucharist. This means that the tradition has held and still holds that a lived out objective contradiction may not always prevail over and against the good of the penitent. . . .

In other words, *Amoris laetitia* recalls that part of the tradition—at its roots, the very same tradition underpinning *Familiaris consortio*—that does not absolutize the criterion but relativizes it and subordinates it to the good of the persons involved. There are, indeed, circumstances in which every norm is redirected to it proper finality which is *salus animarum*, the salvation of souls, and the good of persons.[5]

With careful nuance, Basilio Petrà describes accompaniment and discernment for persons who have divorced and remarried and now

---

5. Basilio Petrà, *Amoris laetitia: accompagnare, discernere e integrare la fragilità—la morale cattolica dopo il capitolo ottavo* (Assisi: Cittadella Editrice, 2016), pp. 22–23 (translation mine).

seek to be integrated into the life of the Church, including, if possible, the sacramental life of the Church with absolution and the Eucharist. Petrà's treatment does not signal a capitulation to situation ethics or consequentialism or, even more significantly, a retreat on the Church's doctrine concerning the permanence and indissolubility of marriage. He upholds the objective values and convictions, as he ought. At the same time, he brings to bear the wisdom of the practical moral tradition in applying these values and convictions to particular situations or cases in a process of accompaniment and discernment, whether in the nonsacramental internal forum or the sacramental forum. When Petrà does this, he stands in a great and solid moral tradition that can count among its leading lights St. Alphonsus Maria de Liguori and other *auctores probati* [proven and reliable theologians]. From another perspective, Petrà and those engaged in direct pastoral ministry are exercising that formational task as we have come to understand it in the context of *Amoris laetitia*. That formation means the formation of people trying to be faithful disciples. It is not a reformation of the doctrinal and moral tradition. It does mean a step forward in greater fidelity to the Gospel.

Step 6: Toward greater fidelity. In certain cases—and that word "certain" needs to be underscored to recognize that what transpires in accompaniment and discernment is not a general practice but a particular one—those who are divorced and remarried can be given absolution and admitted to the Eucharist. In these instances, one might be tempted to say that they have passed a threshold and that they have arrived where they should be. That assessment, however, would amount to a major misunderstanding.

As long as we walk this earth, our journey of discipleship continues. As long as we live in this life, we are continually summoned to greater and greater fidelity and a more and more generous surrender to the Lord. This is certainly true for those couples who are in complex situations. Even if after careful discernment they are integrated into the life of the Church and participate in the sacraments, they are still summoned to never lose sight of the ideal and to strive earnestly to reach it. This process belongs to that formational journey of discipleship that we considered earlier. Pope Francis cites the final synod report to this effect when he speaks of the Church's responsibility: "'The church has the responsibility of helping them [these couples] understand the divine pedagogy of grace in their lives and offering them assistance so they can reach the fullness of God's plan for them,' something that is always possible by the power of the Holy Spirit" (297). Practically, the Holy Father's words mean that the formational ministry of accompaniment and discernment, in some form or another, ought to continue for the couple. This ministry will help them to keep discovering the new ways that God is calling them forward. Pope Francis recapitulates his thoughts in these words: "Let us recall that this discernment is dynamic; it must remain ever open to new stages of growth and to new decisions that can enable the ideal to be more fully realized" (303).

Step 7: Avoiding scandal. Instances of divorced and remarried couples connecting or reconnecting with the Church pose a particular challenge. Pope Francis, citing the synod report, describes the challenge in this way: "The baptized who are divorced and civilly remarried need to be more fully integrated into Christian communities in the variety of ways possible, while avoiding any occasion of scandal" (299). The avoidance of scandal is, indeed, a pastoral and personal challenge. *Scandalum* means stumbling block, something that disables others from embracing the fullness of faith.

Concerning divorced and remarried couples who are, or want to be, integrated into the life of the Church, the possibility of scandal cuts in two ways. To block people entirely from participation in the life of the Church is a scandal, because it is clearly a counterwitness to the mercy of God. Pope Francis says: "No one can be condemned forever, because that is not the logic of the gospel!" (297). At the same time, the integration of these couples into the life of the Church can be perceived as watering down the demands of the Gospel. That, too, must be avoided. "To show understanding in the face of exceptional situations never implies dimming the light of the fuller ideal or proposing less than what Jesus offers to the human being" (307).

Regarding scandal, there are three constituencies: the couple themselves, the ministers of the Church, and the people in the pew. A couple that has engaged in a process of discernment and has come to a certain level of participation in the life of the Church does not owe any form of public accounting. They are not obligated to share the personal details of their situation. At the same time, they may be obligated to a certain discretion to avoid misunderstandings. The words "certain discretion" mean exactly that. For example, whatever might suggest flaunting their exceptional status ought to be avoided. That does not mean, however, monitoring and adjusting every behavior because of its possible impact on others in the community.

The ministers of the Church ought to invite the faithful to embrace the full ideal of marriage and family life that the Gospel proposes. They ought to regularly remind other believers to reserve judgment, especially concerning situations for which they do not have knowledge or responsibility.

Finally, the community needs to monitor itself and cut short any judgments based on impressions. There ought to be a kind of latitude that gives room for people to participate in the life of the Church without arousing suspicions about motives and proper status. Of course, this kind of patient forbearance that trusts the good will of people and the wisdom of community leadership also ought to be balanced with a concern to helpfully challenge others to live out the Gospel to the fullest.

Avoiding scandal means far more than making sure that behavior conforms to rules. It recognizes that we have a responsibility to each other to foster growth in the Christian life without making judgments about the behaviors or motives of others.

Step 8: Moving forward. This last step recapitulates everything that has gone before. The motivation for caring for the divorced and remarried is the desire to see that their spiritual lives go forward. The Church cannot and ought not to leave them to their own devices or simply tell them that they have missed the mark. One of the great messages that permeates *Amoris laetitia* is hope for everyone, no matter their situation. God does not abandon us, and the Church, walking in the footsteps of Jesus, cannot abandon people, no matter how complicated their situation.

How this accompaniment occurs is very important. That is why, in light of *Amoris laetitia*, we have differentiated eight steps and why we have not been content to offer generalizations. This accompaniment means a genuine investment in the lives of people and an infusion of hope for them. It will always respect the particularities of their lives and never be content to offer a generic solution.

☀ Questions for Reflection

1. How can the meaning of conscience be explained simply?

2. How does conscience help people claim personal responsibility?

3. Why is accompaniment so important, especially when conscience tries to decipher the more complicated part of our life journey?

7

Formation in Community: Challenges of Implementation for the Church

> I encourage Christian communities to recognize the great benefit that they themselves receive from supporting engaged couples as they grow in love.
>
> —*Amoris laetitia, 207*

At the very beginning of *Amoris laetitia*, Pope Francis informs readers that he is not offering a last word on every question surrounding marriage and family life (2). As the fruit of two synods and a worldwide consultation with families, the exhortation concludes a particular process and at the same time launches efforts for the Church to claim and reclaim ways of serving marriages and family life. The exhortation invites us to take up formational challenges that will help us move into the future.

A particular challenge is how to provide formation in community for marriages and families. Communities already provide married couples and their families with spiritual formational resources, but they need to focus and strengthen their efforts. Chapter 6, "Some Pastoral Perspectives," points to a number of directions that need to be taken up to foster the spiritual formation of marriages and families. These directions, it should be noted, are more indications than plans for fully developed programs.

Parishes

Citing the final report of the synod, Pope Francis writes: "The main contribution to the pastoral care of families is offered by the parish, which is the family of families" (202). The Holy Father identifies the crucial contribution that parishes make to marriages and families. He speaks of "pastoral care," which can be understood as spiritual formation. He also affirms that this care happens in a parish that is "the family of families." In the paragraph, he notes that priests and other pastoral ministers need a much better formation to serve families. He identifies the clear challenge to equip and form parish ministers to carry on their responsibilities. Embedded in his words is the significant challenge to develop a parish as a family of families.

How exactly can a parish be the family of families? Here and there, it is possible to find tight-knit communities that are aware of their parish as a family of families. This seems to be rare. In urban settings, for example, parishes are more marked by anonymity than familial intimacy. If parishes are to be the main contributors to the care of families precisely as the family of families, there is work to be done. Pastoral leadership and the people in the pews will need to find ways to configure their life together, so that it does indeed reflect a family of families.

Marriage Preparation

In paragraph 206, Pope Francis once again cites the synod report concerning marriage preparation. This paragraph offers a vision of what could be and ought to be the shape of marriage preparation for couples. Envisioning the community intimately involved in that preparation, it states:

> In this regard, the Synod Fathers agreed on the need to involve the entire community more extensively by stressing the witness of families themselves and by grounding marriage preparation in the process of Christian initiation by bringing out the connection between marriage, baptism, and the other sacraments. The Fathers also spoke of the need for specific programs of marriage preparation aimed at giving couples a genuine experience of participation in ecclesial life and a complete introduction to various aspects of family life.

Notice how this recommendation and direction fit with an understanding of the essential elements of spiritual formation. That formation involves a journey as well as accompaniment and shared discernment. All of this fits perfectly with a model drawn from Christian initiation (the Rite of Christian Initiation of Adults) for marriage preparation. It summons the community to participate and contribute to this moment in the life of a couple preparing for marriage.

Although there may be places where this vision of marriage preparation is implemented, it is not an ordinary pattern. This vision of the synod is a challenge to develop something new.

Accompanying the First Years of Married Life

A significant section of chapter 6 (217–230) is dedicated to accompanying couples in the first years of married life. This stage of their relationship is especially important because it can have lasting impact in shaping the rest of their life together. Newly and recently married couples meet a number of challenges and opportunities in short order. If they do so alone, they are at a disadvantage. The gist of this section is to note the importance of the first years and to invite the community to take up the task and responsibility of accompaniment.

Again in this vision, the faith community, perhaps best represented by older experienced couples, offers an essential contribution to the formation of younger couples who want to solidify their relationship. It should be noted that this pattern is not something that is in place. The challenge is to develop ways of providing accompaniment for younger couples and so nourish their spiritual formation.

Welcoming New Life

Chapter 5 of *Amoris laetitia* focuses on the theme "Love Made Fruitful." The chapter considers what it means to bring new life into the world and how this is essentially connected to the love of the spouses. The writing of Pope Paul VI and John Paul II have developed the Church's teaching on openness to life in marriage. The vision is ample and necessary in our time and culture, when the generative dimension of marriage often falters. This chapter of *Amoris laetitia* assumes the previous teaching and moves, as other parts of the exhortation do, in the direction of formation. Implicit in that formation is the presence of a faith community that is present to married couples.

The decision to have children is, of course, deeply personal. At the same time, a couple makes this intimate decision in a community context. As Pope Francis indicates, they should be able to count on an extended family. That extended family exercises a formative function by sharing experience and offering reliable support to a couple. The larger community has an interest in the new life generated in a marriage. When parents bring their children for Baptism, they also build up the Body of Christ.

※ Questions for Reflection

1. *Amoris laetitia* refers to the parish as a "family of families." How can parishes help members think of their faith community this way?

2. Do your parish families see themselves as connected to the other families?

3. How could a parish begin to accompany young married couples?

8

The Formation of Conscience

We should not be trapped into wasting our energy
in doleful laments but rather seek new forms of
missionary creativity.

—Amoris laetitia, 57

Struggle and Victory in Christian Family Life

The apostolic exhortation is about the formation of disciples in the context of marriage and family life. The Church fosters and facilitates this formation. At every stage, the Church must also help believers to grapple with the dimension of struggle in their lives. Struggle takes different forms for all of us. I may, for example, struggle to know and do the right thing or the better thing in my life. I may struggle to identify the larger direction of my life, as God wants me to live it out. I may struggle with self-centeredness and other sinful tendencies that keep me from fully surrendering myself into God's hands. I may struggle to love myself and others as Jesus has loved us. These are just a sample of struggles that Christian disciples may face on their journey.

St. Paul shares his struggle in a passage from his letter to the Romans:

> I do not understand my own actions. For I do not do what I want, but I do the very thing I hate. . . . For I know that nothing good dwells within me, that is, my flesh. I can will what is right, but I cannot do it. For I do not do the good I want, but the evil I do not want is what I do. Now if I do what I do not want, it is no long I that

do it, but sin that dwells within me. . . . Wretched man that I am! Who will rescue me from this body of death? Thanks be to God through Jesus Christ our Lord! (Romans 7:15, 18-20, 24-25)

Notice several important aspects of Paul's experience. First, he is engaged in a true struggle. That struggle is not only with himself but also with movements beyond him. The last word in the struggle, however, is not defeat but victory in Jesus Christ.

In an earlier study on the devil,[1] I attempted to retrieve and articulate the work of the devil embedded in the ordinary course of daily life and correlatively the prospect of our victory over sin and evil in Jesus Christ. The devil is a real presence in Scripture and in our experience. The devil is the presence that seeks to pull us away from God and the things of God. Through temptation, the devil tries to derail our journey to God. These subversive maneuvers apply to marriage and family life, especially in the context of *Amoris laetitia.*

The essential dimensions of love in marriage and family life represent the scaffolding, or the inner holding structure, of the marriage itself and the family. Four essential pieces belong to this scaffolding: *truth, unity, mission,* and *hope.* The first element on which love in a marriage and family rests is truth. Although truth ought to be simple, in marriages and families it is multidimensional. There is the truth of God, of self, and of honest relationships. The second element, unity, is a natural component of marriage and family. Although unity would seem to be an obvious part of the scaffolding of love, it also carries a complexity captured in the word "communion." The unity of family communion joins the individuality and specificity of each person in a dynamic tension with their interlocking relationships. The third element, mission, expresses the purpose of marriage and family life. Mission has both an internal and external component. In other words, there is a purposeful direction internal to the life of the marriage and family. Generally, that is the building and cultivation of the intimate

---

1. Louis J. Cameli, *The Devil You Don't Know: Recognizing and Resisting Evil in Everyday Life* (Notre Dame, IN: Ave Maria Press, 2011).

relationships that bind people together. There is also an external mission or purpose. Catholic social teaching affirms that the family is the basic cell or unit of society. Finally, the fourth element is hope. No individual, no marriage, no family, and no society can move forward without a sense of hope that gives us a promised future as our horizon for living and acting. Hope in marriages and families sustains a double movement forward for the family itself and for the world that so depends on families.

If the major scaffolding of marriages and families and their sustaining love is found in truth, unity, mission, and hope, then surely the adversary will be bent on weakening, or even dismantling, these elements. Indeed, that is the case. In daily life, the devil's major works are deception, division, diversion, and discouragement. The great struggles and temptations of spouses and family members are to be found in deception against truth, division against unity, diversion against mission, and discouragement against hope.

The Church's responsibility to married couples and to their families includes providing essential resources as they face the inevitable struggles of their lives together. What are the essential resources to help marriages and families in their struggles?

Teaching that draws on the wisdom of the faith tradition helps people to recognize what they face in their struggles. The accompaniment that is so prominent in the exhortation is also another resource. Most importantly, the Church brings Jesus Christ to these marriages and families. With Word, sacrament, and community life, the Church gives struggling people the means to recognize their ultimate victory in Christ.

A Summary of the Fourfold Spiritual Struggle

Deception. In its opening chapters, the Bible portrays the devil's deceptive ploys. To the first woman, the devil, appearing as a serpent, says, "You will not die; for God knows that when you eat of it your eyes will be opened, and you will be like God, knowing good and evil" (Genesis 3:4–5). This is a lie coupled with a false promise, and it works to trick Adam and Eve. Deception takes on various forms. It can bend language and it can complicate things so thoroughly that the truth of a given situation can scarcely be known or remedied. Deception provides protective cover for inconvenient truths.

Division. The *diabolos* is quite literally the one who engages in *dia-ballein*, the action of splitting, fracturing, and dividing. This dynamic of division ranges over many situations. There is the divided self that Paul describes: "For I do not do the good I want, but the evil I do not want is what I do" (Romans 7:19). There are also social divisions, with people pitted against each other. Even in the Church, Paul notes, these divisions occur: "For, to begin with, when you come together as a church, I hear that there are divisions among you" (1 Corinthians 11:18). Finally, there are institutionalized divisions that become embedded in a culture. We are sadly familiar with racism, sexism, ethnocentrism, homophobia, classism, and other kinds of divisions at this level that pull apart the social fabric.

Diversion. The classic story of diversion is the narrative of the temptations of Jesus. The tempter wants to pull Jesus off course. The evangelists clearly indicate Jesus' commitment as loyal Son of his heavenly Father and his willingness to be a suffering Messiah who will heal and liberate through his suffering. As we hear the suggestions of the devil—to turn stones into bread, to worship Satan himself to gain power, and to throw himself off the parapet of the temple in a dazzling display of self-promotion—all of them suggest another path. They are a major diversion of mission.

Discouragement. The last work of the adversary is discouragement, and it is often associated with the experience of acedia in the history of Christian spirituality. Acedia fuels a feeling of frustration with the lack of spiritual progress that leads to retreat from the spiritual journey, turning to something else, or collapsing into paralyzing sadness. Acedia affects good and dedicated people who are on an intentional spiritual journey. It also can affect communities on collective journeys, as it did the Israelites who traveled from the slavery of Egypt to the Promised Land. Acedia is the most dangerous temptation because discouragement can lead people to abandon their journey entirely.

Amoris laetitia Addresses Struggle and Temptation

Some select passages of *Amoris laetitia* illustrate how the exhortation deals with struggle and temptation. As always, the exhortation takes a realistic view of the experience of marriage and family life. In the end, it draws readers into a deeper sense of hope because of the grace of Jesus Christ that is at work in our lives.

Deception
SACRED WORDS

> At times, the couple does not grasp the theological and spiritual import of the words of consent that illuminate the meaning of all the signs that follow. It needs to be stressed that these words cannot be reduced to the present; they involve a totality that includes the future: "until death do us part." The content of the words of consent makes it clear that "freedom and fidelity are not opposed to one another." (*Amoris laetitia*, 214)

A couple vows their love and fidelity to each other at the beginning of a marriage. It is a pledge of consent that signals their intent. They use words as the vehicle to convey their meaning. That initial exchange of vows marks the beginning of the marriage, but other pledges follow across the lifetime of the marriage, promises that sustain and develop the original commitment. At every point, the words of promise must conform to the truth of what the spouses intend. Outright simulation is a possibility, but the more likely danger is to be found in hedging, limiting, and qualifying commitments without transparency. In other words, to protect themselves or to hedge against future possibilities, spouses can succumb to deception by not embracing the whole truth. This has corrosive effects that can eventually rub out the relationship. In their internal communication, spouses must say what they mean and mean what they say. Maintaining that level of consistency and transparency is not an automatic given but requires continuous scrutiny and reaffirmation.

> If someone flaunts an objective sin as if it were part of the Christian ideal or wants to impose something other than what the church teaches, he or she can in no way presume to teach or preach to others; this is a case of something that separates from the community (cf. Mt 18:17). Such a person needs to listen once more to the Gospel message and its call to conversion. (*Amoris laetitia*, 297)

Our culture poses a significant challenge for those who want to embrace a true and authentic understanding of marriage and family life. That challenge is the cultural inclination to establish subjective judgments as the last word. In this passage from *Amoris laetitia*, Pope Francis addresses the danger of bending the truth that is part of the received tradition to conform to a personal judgment. Convictions, especially about marriage and family, that lead to a new way of living need to be grounded in the received tradition of faith.

Division
THE CHALLENGE OF UNION AND COMMUNION

> The idyllic picture presented in Psalm 128 is not at odds with a bitter truth found throughout sacred Scripture, that is, the presence of pain, evil, and violence that break up families and their communion of life and love. For good reason Christ's teaching on marriage (cf. Mt 19:3–9) is inserted within a dispute about divorce. The word of God constantly testifies to that somber dimension already present at the beginning, when, through sin, the relationship of love and purity between man and woman turns into domination: "Your desire shall be for our husband, and he shall rule over you" (Gn 3:16). (*Amoris laetitia*, 19)

At the beginning of *Amoris laetitia*, Pope Francis addresses the forces of division that threaten union and communion in marriage and family. He alludes to this same possibility elsewhere, for example, when he speaks of the shadow side of human sexuality that can introduce violence, manipulation, and domination in the sacred relationship of marriage (153–157). Humanity's proto-history (Genesis 1–11) is filled with examples, many of them drawn from family relationships, that illustrate the way that division and even destruction can invade the closest relationships. Think of Cain and Abel. The ideal of union and communion is tested. And that is the reality.

Diversion
THE CHALLENGE AND STRUGGLE OF HOLDING TO THE MISSION

> The ideal of marriage, marked by a commitment to exclusivity and stability, is swept aside whenever it proves inconvenient or tiresome. The fear of loneliness and the desire for stability and fidelity exist side by side with a growing fear of entrapment in a relationship that could hamper the achievement of one's personal goals. (*Amoris laetitia*, 34)

From our considerations of the formative side of marriage and family life, the reality and experience of process or journey became abundantly clear. Our lives in marriage and family have a purposeful direction or mission. The challenge and the struggle, however, is to sustain the journey in its proper direction or true mission across time. At different moments and for different reasons, as Pope Francis indicates in this short passage, we may feel tempted to fall off the course and so to be diverted from our true purpose.

Discouragement
THE CHALLENGE AND STRUGGLE OF DISCOURAGEMENT
AND FINDING A RESPONSE

> We have often been on the defensive, wasting pastoral energy on denouncing a decadent world without being proactive in proposing ways of finding true happiness. Many people feel that the church's message on marriage and family do not clearly reflect the preaching and attitudes of Jesus, who set forth a demanding ideal and yet never failed to show compassion and closeness to the frailty of individuals like the Samaritan woman or the woman caught in adultery. (*Amoris laetitia*, 38)

The situations that concern us are challenges. We should not be trapped into wasting our energy in doleful laments but rather seek new forms of missionary creativity. (*Amoris laetitia*, 57)

In chapter 2 of *Amoris laetitia* ("The Experiences and Challenges of Families"), Pope Francis outlines a formidable series of challenges that marriages and families face. Among them are a distorted notion of personal freedom, fears about permanent commitment, narcissism, economic hardship, the commercialization of sexuality, especially with pornography, the lack of affordable housing, migration, drug use, violence in families, and the ill treatment of women. Any one of these experiences could trigger a profound sense of discouragement, and clustered together—as they often are in today's world—they can breed a deep-rooted hopelessness about marriage and family life. With that temptation to discouragement comes a twofold challenge: to individuals and families to sustain their journey with confidence and to the Church to find the right way to minister to those in these difficult circumstances. The second challenge belongs to the Church as she tries to minister to those tempted by discouragement. As we read paragraphs 38 and 57 of *Amoris laetitia*, we begin to see a way for the Church to serve the disheartened and the discouraged.

Formative Ministry to Those Who Struggle in Marriage and Family Life

The Church's ministry to married couples and to families certainly belongs to the designated ministers of the Church, ordained ministers, and nonordained ministers. Prompted by the synods on the family, Pope Francis identifies families themselves as primary ministers to families. He writes: "The Synod Fathers emphasized that Christian families, by the grace of the sacrament of matrimony, are the principal agents of the family apostolate, above all through 'their joy-filled witness as domestic churches'" (200). Consequently, whatever we say about formative ministry to those who struggle in marriage and family life applies to all recognized ministers in the Church and families themselves who are blessed with their calling to serve others.

There are five essential moments of ministry to those who struggle in the context of marriage and family. This ministry assumes that whenever necessary and appropriate, the ordinary human means are employed to address struggles. Such ordinary means may include psychological counseling, financial advising, and medical consultations. The direct concern here has to do with struggles that have a spiritual impact on a marriage or a family. In these situations, ministry serves to form and help people to respond to their struggles. It does not replace the freedom of individuals and communities in making their proper decisions. Rather, it enables, empowers, and encourages them to move forward. Consider now the five essential moments of ministry to struggling couples and families.

1. Name. The first moment of formative ministry is to name the human experience of struggle in whatever form it takes. This naming is essential, because it allows people to recognize what they are grappling with. That recognition is foundational for any decisions or directions.

2. Proclaim. To proclaim means moving from the human experience of struggle to the faith experience of our victory in Jesus Christ. In the face of deception, we proclaim Jesus, who breaks the shackles of deception and is "the way, and the truth, and the life" (John 14:6). In the face of division, we proclaim Jesus, who is our peace and unity: "For he is our peace; in his flesh he has made both groups into one and has broken down the dividing wall, that is, the hostility between us" (Ephesians 2:14). In the face of diversion, we proclaim Jesus, who is unstintingly faithful to the mission entrusted to him by the Father: "for I have come down from heaven, not to do my own will but the will of him who sent me" (John 6:38). In the face of discouragement, we proclaim Jesus dwelling within us as pledge of our future: "God chose to make known how great among the Gentiles are the riches of the glory of this mystery, which is Christ in you, the hope of glory" (Colossians 1:27).

The proclamation of Jesus as truth, unity, fidelity to mission, and hope is not simply a counterpoint to deception, division, diversion, and discouragement. It is the key that unlocks dilemmas and creates new possibilities for life beyond the struggles. The powerful Word proclaimed has a creative force to make all things new.

3. Discern. To discern and to help others discern, as we have seen, means taking our human experience and our faith experience (the proclamation described earlier) and holding them together. Discernment is not a rational process of figuring things out. Rather it attunes us to wait and watch and allow God's truth to emerge from the situation. Discernment also means sorting out the feelings, thoughts, and movements that may be swirling about to identify what is of God and what is not of God. The fruit of discernment is a direction or path that, as best as we can understand it, mirrors conformity with what God wants of us.

4. Accompany. Accompaniment means walking with each other as we come to terms with what God desires. Paul's words echo this meaning of accompaniment, when he says, "for we walk by faith, not by sight" (2 Corinthians 5:7). We extend to each other a personal and community, or ecclesial, presence. That presence signals confirmation of a direction, encouragement, and a willingness to help in whatever way is needed. In the context of the spiritual struggles of marriage and family life, this formative ministry of accompaniment is especially important. It draws us away from the temptation to isolation in our struggle as well as from the temptation to fall into our subjective judgments. Accompaniment that enables people to move forward in the middle of misunderstanding and difficulties is the way of Jesus. He walks with two struggling disciples on the way to Emmaus (Luke 24:13–35). He offers words of clarification and—even more significantly—his reassuring presence that enables the disciples to take up a new and transformed direction.

5. Hope. In the middle of our struggles, hope is the air that we breathe to carry on. Without hope, we collapse into our struggle whatever it might be. With hope, we can move forward without fear and without disillusionment. St. Paul says: "and hope does not disappoint us, because God's love has been poured into our hearts through the Holy Spirit that has been given to us" (Romans 5:5). A formative ministry to people who struggle in marriage and family life will always hold up hope so they may move forward. In a particular way, that affirmation of hope is rooted in the mercy of God. Pope Francis speaks of the logic of God's mercy, which can never withdraw from the human condition, even at its darkest edges. This is the deep source of hope. He writes:

> We cannot forget that "mercy is not only the working of the Father; it becomes a criterion for knowing who his true children are. In a word we are called to show mercy because mercy was first shown to us." This is not sheer romanticism or a lukewarm response to God's love, which always seeks what is best for us, for "mercy is the very foundation of the church's life. All her pastoral activity should be caught up in the tenderness that she shows believers; nothing in her preaching and her witness to the world can be lacking in mercy." *(Amoris laetitia,* 310)

Because of the triumph of God's mercy, we have hope even in the most desperate circumstances. We serve hope-in-the-struggle whenever we give witness to God's triumphant mercy, and so enable people to go forward.

☼ Questions for Reflection

1. What sustains you during struggles within your closest relationships?

2. How have you witnessed division slowly creep into what had been a close family?

3. How might that division have been stopped at the beginning?

9

The Domestic Church

The family lives its spirituality precisely by being at one
and the same time a domestic church and a vital cell for
transforming the world.

—Amoris laetitia, 324

Amoris laetitia and the Domestic Church

In *Amoris laetitia*, Pope Francis refers to the family as the "domestic
church." He writes: "St. John Paul II devoted special attention to the
family in his catecheses on human love, in his letter to families,
Gratissimam sane, and particularly in his apostolic exhortation
Familiaris consortio. In these documents the pope defined the family as 'the way of the church'" (69). Later, he situates families at the
heart of the Church: "The church is a family of families, constantly
enriched by the lives of all those domestic churches" (87). Finally, Pope
Francis observes the mission and ministry of families in the context of
the larger Church: "The synod Fathers emphasized that Christian families, by the grace of the sacrament of matrimony, are the principal
agents of the family apostolate, above all through 'their joy-filled witness as domestic churches'" (200).

Although Pope Francis highlights the centrality of the family as
domestic church, he does not offer in the exhortation itself a sustained
development of what this means or what it might look like. It is important to address this missing piece of development. The overall direction
of *Amoris laetitia* shifts what has been until now a dominant

preoccupation with the macro church to a new or renewed focus on the micro church in the family. There is some urgency, then, in developing a better sense of what the domestic church means and looks like.

In the pages that follow, I will offer a sketch of the *ecclesia domestica*, or domestic church, as a prelude to reimaging the Church from the perspective of the family. What follows is a recasting of an earlier essay on the nature of the domestic church.

The Domestic Church at the Center

My mother died in 1986, but she is still a steady presence in my life. In the middle of my sometimes heady theological writing, I hear her voice summoning me to be more realistic. For example, in preparing something on the experience of the domestic church, I came across this statement in the *Catechism of the Catholic Church* that draws from other documents: "The Christian family constitutes specific revelation and realization of ecclesial communion, and for this reason it can and should be called a *domestic church*" (2204).

I know how she would react to this statement. "Did the people who wrote these words ever live in a family? Do they know about kids who cry and fight with each other? Do they know about barking dogs and husbands with exasperating habits? Do they know about bills to pay, laundry to do, meals to prepare, and schedules to coordinate? You call this a church?" Her point is well taken. The domestic church is alive in the rough and tumble of family life as it is lived, not as it is idealized.

Two sentences in the *General Directory for Catechesis*, 255, can launch our reflection on that identity. The *Directory* states:

> The family is defined as a "domestic church," that is, in every Christian family the different aspects and functions of the life of the entire church may be reflected: mission; catechesis; witness; prayer etc. Indeed in the same way as the church, the family "is a place in which the Gospel is transmitted and from which it extends" (*Evangelii nuntiandi*, 71).

These words from the *General Directory* indicate that the family, if it is to be a true domestic church, must embody and reflect the essence of the life of the Church overall. Three words capture that essence: "Word," "sacrament," and "mission." The life of the Church is understood in many ways, for example, her origin in the mystery of the death and Resurrection of the Lord and the binding power of the Holy Spirit that sustains her. In our ordinary experience, however, we live out our lives in the Church through Word, sacrament, and mission. How, then, do Word, sacrament, and mission shape the Christian family and nurture its life as a domestic church?

The Word of God in the Family

For most of us, the family is the place where the Word of God is first proclaimed, received, and studied. *Lumen gentium* declares that "parents . . . are the first heralds of the faith with regard to their children" (11). Ideally, a family would regularly read the Bible together, for example, a short selection before the evening meal. Most often, however, the Word is proclaimed much less formally by telling the story of Jesus and Mary and of the saints, as they are celebrated throughout the liturgical year.

Once proclaimed and received, that Word is also assimilated and studied but not in an academic way. Formation in the Word of God, as the *General Directory* describes it, is "a Christian education more witnessed to than taught, more occasional than systematic, more ongoing and daily than structured into periods" (255). That description reflects the way families live their faith. If the Word of God will have a place in the family, it will probably be around the kitchen table. Beyond that informal encounter with the Word, parents can appropriately foster their family's contact with God's Word through deliberate and regular reminders about the Word of God that they offer to family members. In this way, they proclaim the Word.

Catechesis is a more explicit and deliberate exposure to the Word of God and its implications for living. Catechesis belongs to the whole Church, and in special moments it belongs particularly to the domestic church. This happens, for example, when parents and others teach young children how to pray, when they educate their moral conscience in the context of decision-making, or when they help prepare them to receive the Sacraments of Penance, Eucharist, and Confirmation. The domestic church collaborates with the local faith community or parish in fulfilling its catechetical responsibilities to assimilate and understand the Word of God.

The domestic church does not have limited concerns bounded by the walls of its home. The domestic church shares the expansive vision and direction of the entire Church. In relationship to the Word, this means that the Word of God cannot be simply contained within the family. The family must be in service to bringing the Word to the world. In other words, evangelization is an essential ingredient of the domestic church as it is for the Church overall. In the words of Pope Paul VI, "Evangelizing is in fact the grace and vocation proper to the church, her deepest identity. She exists in order to evangelize."[1] This is no less true of the domestic church, which must be ready through witness and explicit proclamation to alert the world to the Gospel of Jesus Christ. This does not mean that the family is a cult-like cell for proselytizing. Rather, the family, in its words and actions, in its hospitality and service, makes its faith transparent to a waiting world so deeply in need of its Savior. Serving food to the poor and decorating the house for Christmas are very different activities, but both are rooted in Jesus, who saves us, and both make him known to the world. In various ways, the domestic church brings the Word of God to the world.

The Sacraments in the Family

THE SACRAMENT OF MATRIMONY AT THE SERVICE OF COMMUNION

The Sacrament of Matrimony is the foundation of the domestic church. The sacrament that joins a man and a woman in a lifelong, exclusive, and indissoluble union that generates new life is the beginning and sustaining force of the church in the home. The Sacrament of

---

1. *Evangelii nuntiandi*, 14.

A New Vision of Family Life

Matrimony has that power because it is, as the *Catechism of the Catholic Church* describes it, one of the sacraments at the service of communion. "Two other sacraments, Holy Orders and Matrimony, are directed towards the salvation of others; if they contribute as well to personal salvation, it is through service to others that they do so. They confer a particular mission in the church and serve to build up the People of God" (1534).

The sacrament sustains the union of husband and wife so that their marriage can foster communion, the union of God's people in knowledge and love that has its roots in the most Holy Trinity, Father, Son, and Holy Spirit. Communion is the hallmark of the Church, which is "in the nature of sacrament—a sign and instrument, that is, of communion with God and of unity among all men."[2] Man and woman joined in the Sacrament of Matrimony serve communion in their very own family and enable it— by God's grace—to be a domestic church. Beyond their particular family, they contribute to communion in the whole Church and, ultimately, in the world.

THE DOMESTIC CHURCH BRINGS ITS MEMBERS TO THE CHURCH FOR SACRAMENTS

The domestic church brings its members to the Church for the celebration of the sacraments. Parents, for example, bring their children for Baptism, Confirmation, Eucharist, and Penance. Not only do they bring their children and so initiate them, but they continue to bring them so that they can fully live the sacramental life of the Church.

That same domestic church pays attention to the admonition in the Letter of James: "Are any among you sick? They should call for the elders of the church and have them pray over them, anointing them with oil in the name of the Lord" (5:14). The domestic church brings its ailing members forward for the Anointing of the Sick. In the final stages of our earthly life, the domestic church calls for the last sacrament, Viaticum, the Eucharist given as the food of travelers who pass

---

2. *Lumen gentium*, 1.

over to eternal life. For these sacraments, often it is the turn of the children to call for the sake of their parents.

Although a vocation to priestly service in the Sacrament of Holy Orders is a grace God gives to an individual, the domestic church serves as a place of preparation and formation for that calling. Similarly, the domestic church encourages and forms its members, who are called to live out their Baptism in consecrated or vowed life.

THE DOMESTIC CHURCH IS WHERE SACRAMENTS ARE LIVED OUT

Sacraments are not merely ritual events celebrated in a moment. They are encounters with the living God manifested in the mystery of Jesus Christ. Those encounters continue beyond the ritual moment, because they initiate us into a new way of living. The domestic church is an important place where the sacraments are lived out. Consider the following examples.

The *Catechism of the Catholic Church* speaks about living out the Sacrament of Baptism in this way: "It is here [in the domestic church] that the father of the family, the mother, children, and all members of the family exercise the *priesthood of the baptized* in a privileged way 'by the reception of the sacraments, prayer and thanksgiving, the witness of a holy life, and self-denial and active charity'" (1657).[3]

Similarly, when a family returns home from the celebration of the Eucharist, they are summoned to live out the self-sacrificing love of Jesus Christ made present in the Mass and which they carry within themselves in virtue of their Holy Communion with him. For those who belong to a family, the primary locus where the self-sacrificing love of Jesus Christ is lived out can only be the domestic church.

Again, when family members have celebrated the Sacrament of Penance and have encountered the merciful forgiveness of God, they not only live gratefully because of God's mercy but they are also summoned to extend God's mercy to others (see Matthew 18:23–35). The primary place where family members will live out the gift of the

---

3. The quotation is from *Lumen gentium*, 10.

A New Vision of Family Life

Sacrament of Penance with its dimensions of healing, reconciliation, and forgiveness will be the domestic church.

THE EXTENSION OF SACRAMENTAL LIFE
IN THE WORSHIP OF THE DOMESTIC CHURCH

The sacramental life of the Church is extended in the liturgy of the domestic church. In other words, the domestic church extends the official public worship of the whole Church in several ways.

The ordinary and common prayer of the domestic church may well be prayer at mealtimes, at night, and possibly in the morning. Other forms of prayer can be important expressions of the liturgy of the domestic church. Devotional prayers, such as the Rosary, have been an important part of many family traditions. The rediscovery of the Liturgy of the Hours as the official daily prayer for the entire Church can lift the level and quality of prayer in the domestic church and link it with the Church universal.[4]

The domestic church provides a place of preparation for and assimilation of the Church's liturgy by offering an opportunity for silence and personal prayer. It is no small task in a busy household to create and sustain—even for a moment—silence or quiet spaces, but it can be done. This allows hearts to be open to what the Church's liturgy will offer and to assimilate more personally what the Church has celebrated.

Finally, the domestic church extends the experience of the Church's sacraments and liturgy by dedicating sacred space in the home and venerating the sacramental images that recall the story of our salvation and the grace that is ours through Jesus Christ. The presence of the saints, the friends of God, and of the angels, his providential emissaries, finds a fresh reminder in images that decorate the home.

---

4. In *Marialis cultus: For the Right Ordering and Development of Devotion to the Blessed Virgin Mary*, 54, Pope Paul VI accords primacy to the Liturgy of the Hours for family prayer but also extols the value of praying the Rosary. He writes: "But there is no doubt that, after the celebration of the Liturgy of the Hours, the high point which family prayer can reach, the Rosary should be considered one of the best and most efficacious prayers in common that the Christian family is invited to recite."

The Mission of the Church Alive in the Family

The mission of the Church is her holy purpose, which the Lord Jesus entrusted to his bride. He gives the Church the great commission to bring the Gospel to all people, to baptize them, and to make them his disciples. He assures his Church that as she carries out this mission, he will be present to her to the end of the age, that is, to the end of time (see Matthew 28:18–20). Because the domestic church reflects the reality of the universal Church, the domestic church shares in the mission. Consider how the family moves beyond itself as a domestic church in mission to the world.

From the very beginning, believing families "were islands of Christian life in an unbelieving world."[5] And from the beginning, that presence has been one of mission and evangelization. The family's witness has never been more important than today. The *Catechism*, 1655, explains the domestic church and its place in the world:

> Christ chose to be born and grow up in the bosom of the holy family of Joseph and Mary. The church is nothing other than "the family of God." From the beginning, the core of the church was often constituted by those who had become believers "together with all [their] household" (Acts 18:8). When they were converted, they desired that "their whole household" should also be saved. These families who became believers were islands of Christian life in an unbelieving world.

The mission of the Church cannot be fulfilled unless men and women who are called to special service respond to their vocation. Parents in the domestic church have a special role to play in the discernment and encouragement of vocations. Speaking of parents, the *Catechism* states: "They should encourage them in the vocation which is proper to each child, fostering with special care any religious vocation" (1656).

The domestic church can fulfill the mission by being an agent of charity, justice, reconciliation, and peace. In a particular way, the care

---

5. *Catechism of the Catholic Church*, 1655.

of the poor ought to become a central and abiding concern for the family that seeks to live out its mission as a domestic church. One of the final blessings in the marriage ritual expresses this aspect of mission clearly: "May you be witnesses in the world to God's charity, so that the afflicted and needy who have known your kindness may one day receive you thankfully into the eternal dwelling of God."[6]

Finally, the domestic church fulfills its mission through the more general work of service and, within that, the particular service of hospitality. The family as domestic church opens its doors to those who need to share in its life. The *Catechism*, 1658, speaks of this service of hospitality in this way:

> Many remain *without a human family*, often due to conditions of poverty. Some live their situation in the spirit of the Beatitudes, serving God and neighbor in exemplary fashion. The doors of homes, the "domestic churches," and of the great family which is the church must be open to all of them. "No one is without a family in this world: the church is a home and family for everyone, especially those who 'labor and are heavy laden.'"

Conclusion

The domestic church is a true instance of the reality of the Church. It participates in those basic and constitutive elements of the Church— Word, sacrament, and mission. The experience of a domestic church obviously looks and feels different from an experience of Church in a parish, a diocese, or at the level of the Church universal. That difference, however, does not signal less importance. The domestic church, for most of us, has provided the doorway and the foundation for our participation in the Church in her larger dimensions. The domestic church has also provided us with the place where we live out our faith most directly day-to-day and most intensely in the rough and tumble of ordinary family life.

---

6. *Order of Celebrating Matrimony*, 77.

✺ Questions for Reflection

1. How do you see the domestic church evangelizing in and outside of the family?

2. What resources can the parish provide the domestic church to help it fulfill its mission?

3. How has *Amoris laetitia* expanded your perspective on the domestic church?